# M<sup>c</sup>GINN
## OF THE CALTON

# MᶜGINN
# OF THE CALTON

The Life and Works
of
Matt MᶜGinn
1928 - 1977

GLASGOW CITY
LIBRARIES

Reprinted 1993

ISBN 0 906169 15 1

Cover photographs by Brian Shuel and Oscar Marzaroli.


Published by Glasgow City Libraries.
The Mitchell Library, North Street, Glasgow G3 7DN.
Typeset by Newtext Composition Ltd., 72 Waterloo Street, Glasgow G2 7DA.
Printed by Bell & Bain Ltd., 303 Burnfield Road, Glasgow G46 7UQ.

# CONTENTS

# FOREWORD

Matt McGinn didn't look like Robert Redford. He looked much better. Physically he was the archetypal Glaswegian of his class and generation: short, stocky and robust; the complexion ruddy, and the rough hewn features surmounted by the tartan bunnet which on anyone else would have looked like affectation, but which was accepted by all as simply an expression of the McGinn personality. Personality and character he had in abundance. He drew people effortlessly to him, and dealt with friends, admirers and critics alike, in the same easy and direct way. He didn't know how to be patronising, and he certainly was not a man to be patronised.

The most frequent criticism levelled at Matt's work was that it lacked polish, and it's true that some of his songs were as roughly textured as the man himself. Perhaps he was in too much of a hurry to be fastidious, and there may even have been a subconscious premonition that his time was not to be long. Sometimes, however, a piece would emerge from the white hot kiln of his creativity, full fired, high glazed, and ready for use. 'Coorie Doon,' or 'The Miner's Lullaby' is a typical McGinn idea; simple but telling. A child huddles in the warmth and security of the cot, while the father huddles in a three foot seam. Deep in the dark he sweats his life away to give life to his child. Sentimental? Not when you heard Matt sing it.

Had he lived longer, his work may indeed have become more honed and polished, but who is to say whether or not it might have lost some of its vigour and immediacy in the process. He was a furious and erratic worker, and no doubt many fragments, ideas, sketches and concepts have been lost, but this long overdue collection will give a sympathetic and comprehensive picture of the man and his work.

Matt McGinn was the genuine article. A working class poet who spoke not only for his own people, but for anyone who shared the McGinn qualities of compassion, humour and humanity. He is very much alive in his music, and in those of us who were lucky enough to know him and to work with him.

*Jimmie Macgregor*

# INTRODUCTION

Matt McGinn was born on January 17th 1928. He was one of a family of 9 having 5 sisters and 3 brothers. The McGinns lived in a two-roomed house in Ross Street at the corner of Gallowgate in the Calton district of Glasgow. Matt died on 6th January 1977 from smoke inhalation after falling asleep with a lighted cigarette in his hand. During his 49 years, Matt McGinn enjoyed a meaningful, worthwhile, action-packed life.

Although his formal schooling ended at the age of 12 when he was sent to an approved school for 2 years, he was an intelligent, well-read man. Always thirsting for knowledge, at the age of 31 Matt gratefully abandoned his shift-work at Guest Keen and Nettlefold in Hillington when he won a Trade Union Scholarship to Ruskin College in Oxford. After obtaining his Diploma in Economics and Political Science, he attended Huddersfield Teachers' Training College and while there won a Sunday newspaper competition for a song in the folk tradition. In his autobiographical stories, Matt relates the hilarious tale of both the song and the editor's horror on being informed by the judges that McGinn's outrageous 'Foreman O'Rourke' – the story of a factory worker who was eventually hanged for the murder by drowning of his unpopular 'gaffer' when he pulled the lavatory plug on him – was the winning song and that as such he was required to publish it.

On completing his studies, Matt returned home to Rutherglen to teach in a variety of schools for three years, after which he worked as organiser of The Gorbals Adventure Playground, the first of its kind in Scotland, before becoming a full-time singer comedian, actor and writer.

In the early 60's the folk-song revival was blossoming in Glasgow. The Anti-Polaris movement was at its height and there were annual Aldermaston Marches. Demonstrators sat down at the Holy Loch to be carted off to the police station in huge claustrophobic furniture vans. Folk singers were very much a part of the protest and Matt was very much a leading folk-singer. While

Teacher at Budhill School, Springboig, c.1963.

the majority of 'folk-songs' were traditional songs, there were now a growing number of contemporary protest, anti-war and anti-Polaris songs and Matt was happily involved in singing and writing these but also learning from the many excellent writers concentrating on this type of song.

Matt's output of songs was prolific at this time. It seemed that no topic of interest escaped a McGinn song. He wrote about life in the factory, life in the Gallowgate, stories and songs about barrow boys, about the problems suffered by 'Footba' Referees', the frustrations of the overtime addict desperate for 'Three Nights and a Sunday' or the other 'right to work' addict and adherent of a '4 day week and a 2 hour day'; the poor teacher demented by a crowd of rowdy children who although opposed in theory to corporal punishment, was driven to enthusiastic support of capital punishment. Matt wrote of the Govan couple whose house was haunted by a Dundee ghost – from the ghost's point of view!

Following the death of his brother Joe, Matt was moved to adapt and add to the work of Joe's favourite poet Omar Khayyam, put it all to music and so from Khayyam's magnificent Rubaiyat was created McGinn's haunting 'Magic Shadow Show'.

9

With guitar, 1962.
Liam Clancy far left.

Given an ideal world and the redistribution of wealth, I for one would vote that all aspiring composers should have a grand piano, be taught to read music, have a little soundproof outhouse some distance from the family home and there compose to their hearts' content. We had none of these things and Matt's method of composing was no doubt somewhat unorthodox. First of all he would have an idea, then words and music would come together. Never, ever, was anything ever noted on paper. He relied on his memory and sang everything aloud line after line, again and again. Often, having heard a new song being sung so many times, the children were well able to prompt Matt, remembering words or tune which he may have forgotten. Worst of all was when he chose to accompany himself on the guitar on which he couldn't play a single note! Most often we silently rejoiced when he would take his current guitar to an engagement and then promptly lose it – which happened frequently.

The crazy, silly song, 'Willie MacNamara' I well remember. The idea came to Matt one Sunday morning. I am sure he was determined to have at least one new song for the concert he was playing in the McLellan Galleries that evening. As was his wont, he repeated line after line, verse after verse about the house all day

As Porter in *Macbeth*, Edinburgh Festival, 1965.

until he remembered the words and tune. What made matters worse this particular day, was the fact that he was so hoarse he could scarcely speak and singing was well-nigh impossible. That evening, exhausted after the busy, noisy day I had endured and anxious about Matt's lack of voice, I went along to the concert with him. Matt was the star turn and as such was due to appear last on the programme. I listened and appreciated the performances of the other singers, admiring the lovely voices and skilful guitar playing and wondered how on earth this wee Glasgow bloke, totally devoid of any musical accompaniment and with a voice which had been described as a mixture of lumpy porridge and broken glass, and which on this occasion was only a few croaks from being non-existent, would fare.

But that night, Matt, ever the showman, concentrated on stories and jokes and soon in the inimitable McGinn fashion had the audience in the palm of his hand. Then, on introducing his latest composition, Matt explained that following the style of his big

With Billy Connolly, Tam Harvey, Danny Kyle and others, UCS rally, Glasgow Green, 1971.                                      Photograph by O. Marzaroli

pal Pete Seeger, he wanted the audience to help him in singing his next song and asked that those with the high voices should sing AARRA while those with the low voices would sing AARRA. (While Pete Seeger specialises in inspiring his chorus-singing audiences to splendid harmonies, Matt's objective was always humorous). So after much ado and dividing the audience into their appropriate singing groups, all of which they responded to with the good natured gusto and enthusiasm that is the reward of the good artist, Matt had them all practising – AARRA – everybody of course singing in just the one key, only to fall into the trap he had set for them when he proceeded to sing in a deep throaty gallus voice:

> There was a wee fella frae the Gallowgate,
> His name it wis Willie MacNam-AARRA
> And the way he earned his living, wis,
> Wae gaen short weight frae a B-AARRA

Even by the end of the first verse the audience were rolling in their seats with laughter and for me all the silly words that I had heard over and over again for the best part of the day took on a new meaning and I was as helpless with laughter as those around me. So despite everything, the old McGinn magic had again triumphed and several hundred people enjoyed a night to remember.

Matt's career as a performer spanned some 15 years. During this time he sang, told stories, spun jokes in Folk Clubs, Concert Halls, Miners' Welfares and Clubs and Pubs, indeed in everything from the local Bingo to Carnegie Hall (yes, in New York), as Matt himself relates in this volume. Matt only needed to read a newspaper report of an industrial dispute before he was on the 'phone offering his services. He sang for workers, not only at concerts for funds, but cheered many many demonstrations when he marched through the streets among the ranks of the workers, singing and calling quick-witted slogans. On these occasions he was marvellously and cheerfully funny and must have uplifted the spirits of many of those at the heart of the dispute. Matt was heavily involved in support of the U C S workers when they took control of their shipyards, and later the workers of the *Scottish Daily News* when they attempted to create their own newspaper from the ashes of the *Scottish Daily Express*. Matt was in fact known as 'The Bard to the Daily News' and it seemed to me that every time the TV flashed a picture of the Daily News workers meeting, there in

At the *Scottish Daily News*, 1975.

the middle was Matt complete with tartan bunnet. Together with our son Matt, he was to the fore in organising and singing in support of the *Daily News*, and today in his home in Germany, young Matt proudly displays a silver mug which is inscribed —

> To Matt and Matt Junior McGinn from
> the workers of the Scottish Daily News
> in appreciation of their support during
> the struggle. March 1975.

Matt was a clever man who used humour very skilfully to puncture holes in pomposity, to flatten cant and hypocrisy and to expose bigotry. All of this is evident in the songs in this book. But he also wrote children's songs, love songs and even some sad songs. In what I consider one of the most moving songs he ever wrote, 'The Ibrox Disaster', he captures the feelings of horror at the awful tragedy – '. . . 66 people died, some in flower of their manhood, when the fences gave way and the barriers bent . . .' – punctuates this with his knowledge of the feelings and attitudes of Glasgow people – '. . . seasoned Glasgow policemen, their faces all tear-stained . . .' – and rounds it all off (even in this seeing hope for change) with '. . . all of Glasgow enjoined for the first time in history, in the Glasgow Cathedral, no Billy, no Dan, but the Old Firm united to pray for the victims . . .'

We sat together that sad night and listened to the first reports of this awful disaster – and Matt wept.

An intensely political person, Matt was totally committed to the overthrow of the present system of society. His realisation and eventual understanding of the divisions in society he beautifully illustrates in his autobiographical stories when he tells of his discussions with his anarchist friend, Robert Lynn.

Well-read, knowledgeable and articulate, Matt at one time or another had membership of many left-wing political parties or groups. But, never one to sit idly back and quietly 'toe the party line' or unquestioningly accept party political dogma, his stays were mostly short lived – but exciting, as you will read.

Raised a devout Catholic, at a young age Matt discarded the idea of God. Matt and I were both atheists, with no belief in the hereafter.

At Matt's funeral service, 'The International', sung by the hundreds of people present, was the last tribute to him. Harry McShane told me later than on only one other occasion in all his 80-odd years had he heard it rendered so movingly. For any who might consider it vital to attach a political label to a political person I am sure Matt would have been happy to have been tagged with any one – or maybe all of – Anarchist, Communist, Socialist, Socialist Republican, Revolutionary.

We were married in July 1950 and had 26 years of what could only be described as a troubled marriage. Despite all our problems I loved the man dearly and had the greatest respect for his

14

honesty, intellect and integrity. Politically and ideologically we were as one, we shared the same views and could almost read each other's mind.

Our life together began at a time of great hope for change, and Matt retained this hope until his death. We were massively supportive of each other and never in the business of compromising our beliefs or our principles. While taking a stand made life rewarding and exciting, it also brought its own problems by way of lost jobs and lack of money. Self-appointed Plumbers' Helpers' Shop Stewards or outspoken semi-skilled wood screw machine men, seldom invite long periods of trouble-free employment! As both of us worked for many years, woven into our family history are many colourful tales related to the abrupt termination of periods of employment!

Indeed, the last time I saw Matt was shortly before his death when he called to offer the moral support I so badly needed while pursuing a claim of Unfair Dismissal, following what I considered was a principled stand I had taken.

Perhaps many 'happy' marriages manage to survive on much less.

We had four children, Anna, Matt, Eleanor and Shonagh and Matt was an adored and adoring father. His love for his children and his fun and happiness with them can be gleaned from such

Glasgow Green, with Anna, Matt junior, Eleanor and Shonagh, 1966.

15

songs as 'Morning Eleanora' and 'Tell Me What the Tea Leaves Tell Me'.

We were devastated when he died. I doubt if we will ever come to terms with the fact that this unique, silly, lovely, eccentric, impulsive, charismatic man is no more.

Matt was so much a Glasgow man that nothing could be more appropriate than that the City of Glasgow should be publishing this volume. I am delighted with the decision of the District Libraries Publications Board and know that the reader will share with me the pleasure in reading this great collection.

Possibly the easiest task we had was deciding a title. At the first meeting I had with Hamish Whyte and Bob McFarlane of the Libraries Publications Board, they quizzed me regarding a story they had heard relating to Matt's attendance at the launching of the *Scottish Daily News*. The story was indeed true and I elaborated on the event.

At the launching of the first issue of the *Scottish Daily News*, and after a somewhat disconcerting evening spent in the company of a miscellaneous assortment of 'celebrities' (including of all things a Tory MP) which had just culminated in a guided tour of the plant, led by Robert Maxwell, Matt was invited to sign the visitors' book.

Immediately ahead of him in the queue of distinguished visitors was Lord MacLeod of Fuinary. On spotting the signature of the noble Lord – 'MacLeod of Fuinary' – Matt immediately dubbed himself 'McGinn of Calton'. We had no hesitation in agreeing that there could only be one title for the book. I know you will enjoy 'McGinn of the Calton', a fitting tribute to an incredible man.

I have very much appreciated the unstinted help given by many people which went far and beyond the call of duty and which was mostly prompted by respect for Matt.

Firstly, my thanks must go to Glasgow District Libraries for their decision to publish. To John Eaglesham, who has made such a marvellous job of notating the music, special thanks for his skill and dedication; thanks also to David Boyd, John McGuire, Erlend Voy and Drummond Wallace for their musical assistance. My thanks to Joe Fisher of the Glasgow Room at The Mitchell for support, interest and wisdom. Deirdre Craig, who copes with an energy and stamina that have to be envied, has my most grateful thanks. Thanks to Appleseed Music, the American friends of Matt McGinn, for their permission to reprint the songs for which they hold the copyright. Oscar Marzaroli and Brian Shuel took many of the fine photographs and to them and all the photographers I am most grateful. A big 'thank you' to Bob McFarlane, Chairman of the Libraries Publications Board, for all his hard work, enthusiasm, kindness and moral support and to Hamish Whyte, who gave unstintingly of his time, his knowledge and his patience to put this book together. Thanks also to the other members of the Board for their help. My thanks must also go to the respective families and spouses of many of the above without whose behind-the-scenes support this book might never have seen the light of day!

*Janette McGinn*
August 1987

At Howwood Inn, c.1972

# Excerpts from Autobiography

## The Gallowgate Calypso

'The three coldest things in the world,' my father said on one occasion, 'are a dog's nose, a man's knees and a woman's arse.'

But on the last account he personally could not have had much to complain about. My mother bore him nine children of which I was the eighth, delivered on The Midwife Special on the Seventeenth of January nineteen twenty eight if we are to believe the birth certificate, and I know of no valid reason for disbelieving the record of the Registrar.

'Oh Mrs McGinn, he's got a lucky cap,' said the nurse and proceeded to take the unbroken caul and place it carefully around a saucer. She had just taken away the last lucky thing I was to have about my face to leave it on the mantlepiece to await the arrival of a sailor. Superstition had it that these cauls could act as charms at sea and that the seaman who had a lucky cap in his possession would never come to any harm. Mine was to prove an exception.

A sailor, Tommy MacCallum, who lived in the Gallowgate heard about this lucky cap, came knocking on the door, paid a sixpence for this piece of unbroken skin, tucked it in an empty shoe polish tin, went off to sea and was drowned three days later.

First memories I suppose have got to be shockers of some kind and mine are of an elder brother then fifteen years old being taken off to the Infirmary with rheumatic fever in an ambulance, and then of his remains being brought home to a very very sad house indeed, to lie for three days before the set-in kitchen bed on trestles. I was three.

We were brought up Catholics and that in Glasgow also meant Celtic supporters and there were plenty of objects and ornaments about the house to indicate to any stranger who came our way what we were at a glance, like holy water fonts, scapulars, pictures of the Sacred Heart and the Virgin and tea plates with pictures of the Celtic team on them.

Our house was a room and kitchen on the ground floor of number eight Ross Street in the Calton district of Glasgow. From both windows we had a magnificent view of a five-horse stable and looming above it the Ham Curer's with, as often as not, the thick black smoke belching from its windows to decorate the other buildings around.

Against these obstacles my mother in common with the majority of neighbours fought a constant battle to keep the house and ourselves spotless. With scrubbing brushes and flycatchers she managed.

The street, with no more than a hundred yards of it, was more like a village, there being in that tiny stretch two pubs and a sweetie shop, a joiner's and a blacksmith's shop, a garage and a Unitarian church which really had no right to be there because there wasn't a Unitarian in the street; there was a gasfitter and plumber's, a sausage casings manufacturer's and a zoo, no less, which still left room for a high class florist, a bookshop, the five-horse stable, a grocer's, the back end of a foundry and a Women's Model Lodging House; and there were five hundred of us living in one-, two- and three-roomed houses in three-storey tenements.

The walls of those tenements had a story to tell. The story of births, marriages and deaths, or, as my mother called them, hatches, matches and despatches. As children we played in that street at 'Shops' and Release the Box and Kick the Can and cards and rounders and boxing and singing and peever and moshie and kicking doors after we'd tied them with string to some other neighbours' door and at guesses and at all kinds of races and we had to be good runners from the police who haunted the street.

Then too there were the sights around the pubs and the model lodging house where the Bad Men came from afar to look for the Bad Women of the 'Model', sights which I tried to recapture in one of my songs, 'The Gallowgate Calypso'.

The names of the policemen in the song were genuine. 'Eat the Moose' who was one of the very few reasonable policemen who came around the area was so called after he had confided to a local shopkeeper that while in the trenches in France 'Ah ate a moose' and John the B, who was severely beaten up in the area on one occasion, was so called because he was a proper one.

We had a picture of Canon O'Reilly in the house. It hung beside the mantlepiece, commanding as proud a place as that of the Blessed Virgin, of Christ bleeding on the Cross or even that of the Celtic Team in full colours which graced an ornamental plate beside the set-in bed.

Canon O'Reilly, although before my time, was a legend in the Gallowgate. A legend of a walking stick and a canon's hat bursting upon the youths and young men in the area and bashing them physically in an unholy effort to break up coin tossing and card schools and games of football which were favourite pastimes.

He would lash out regardless of the religion of his victims, safe in the knowledge that most of them had been baptised Catholics. He was fortified in the wisdom that no one would hit him back if only because there were stories credited as true by the local Catholics that such and such a man had a bad leg simply because he had tried to kick a priest, the crippled limb being an immediately inflicted Act of God! One poor man's arm was permanently stationed parallel with his shoulder because the Lord (so it was said) had not been at all pleased by his attempt to take a punch at one of the clergy.

These Acts of God were speculative, but there was no speculation regarding the violent sorties of Canon O'Reilly into the closes and backcourts of Ross Street, Kent Street, Bain Street, the Gallowgate and Well Street.

Irish accents were rare, most of the populace speaking with the Glasgow Glottal Stop, but the names left no doubt as to the genealogical origin of the Dochertys, Donnellys, Reillys, Connollys or the Quinns.

I was a firm believer in the religion of my forbears, or at least the more recent among them; the more recent among them because those further back — before the legendary Saint Patrick — were pagans and heathens and indeed appear to have been as content with these beliefs as their successors became with theirs. It is worthy of recall that there was an Irish race long before there was any such thing as Christianity.

Then too, I remember Saint Patrick's Day when everyone around wore shamrocks and when, with the half-day holiday we were given, we would go over in droves to Dovehill School and throw other kinds of rocks at the pupils there.

It was impossible also to be unaware of the feverish atmosphere around the Twelfth of July when the Dorises who lived next door would go out in the middle of the night with a pot of paint and brushes and decorate the well at Charlotte Street a proud shade of green and then use the same paint on the red circles of the barber's pole. Then Mrs Makem in the Ham Pend would throw a pail of excrement over her third-storey window at the Orange Walk as it stomped up the Gallowgate. I knew also that there were Protestant hymns which I had heard the Salvation Army women sing of a Sunday in the Ross Street Home for

Females. But I did not really know what all this Protestantism was about, apart from the fact that –

> We'll hang John Knox on the barren rocks,
> With the Sash his father wore!

At the age of five I was severely disappointed and kicked up quite a riot because I could not go to the Protestant school which my pal Colin McConnell was already attending in the Great Dovehill, but had to go to the Catholic School, Saint Alphonsus, in Greendyke Street along with Charlie Logan with whom I had just fallen out over a piece of rope he claimed was his and I claimed was mine because I had seen it first. But I soon got into the religious thing and didn't even use sweary words. When Charlie would sing on our walks down the Glasgow Green:

> Please keep off the grass and let the ladies pass
> Here comes the parkie sliding on his arse,

I would sing bumbaleerie.

I still did not swear, even when we were being taught the catechism, like my older brother Gus had done. Gus was just getting on for seven when the teacher started preparing the class for their First Holy Communion which involved learning the catechism:

'Who made you?'

'God made me'

'Why did God make you?'

'God made me to love him and serve him in this world and be happy with him in the next'

'What is God?'

'God is a supreme spirit'

It was a truly magnificent method of teaching. You did not have to use up too much mental energy in things like thinking. Here you were not only given the question; you were also given the answers and in the exact words.

So the priest was coming round one day to examine the class and see that they had all learned their catechism by heart, and the teacher had allocated all the questions to her pupils to be answered parrot fashion and Gus, who was sitting second from the door in the front row had been given the second question. In the priest

First Communion, 1935.

came and the stupid teacher, forgetting that the boy to whom she had given the first question had just asked with his hand up, permission to 'Leave the room', told the priest to start with the front row from the door. The priest asked Gus, 'Who made you?' 'Please Father,' said Gus standing, 'God didnae make me. God made the boy that's away for a shite.' Needless to say, with this the catechism examination had to halt. Gus was given the belt and my mother was sent for. 'He never learned that language in ma hoose,' said my maw.

I made my First Holy Communion firmly believing in the righteousness of religion and of the Catholic faith in particular. This belief I kept until the age of sixteen when I became as I have remained since a firm atheist with nonetheless a respect for other people's religious leanings. For although I find it almost incredible to see anyone believing that there could be someone with an almighty power in his hands who could allow sickness, famine and war, I nonetheless know that I did in fact believe it for a time so I know such belief is possible in others.


### Rich Man's Paradise

Came the war and my evacuation to one of the poshest districts in Scotland: Newton Mearns, or more specifically to the Broom Estate.

On Saturday September Second 1939, a fleet of buses swooped upon St. Alphonsus' School in Greendyke Street and picked up a straggling mass of children and a handful of mothers, all of us duly ticketed and equipped with a cardboard box containing a gas mask and most with tears trickling down our noses. There had been rumours of war, which to us kids was just an additional bit of excitement, for months now. Splinter shelters and baffle walls were appearing all over the place. The letters A R P for Air Raid Precautions were constantly used in newspapers and in adult conversations which you heard. My da sprang some joke about a man who got his shirt back from the laundry to discover the letters A R P stitched to the tail. When asked for an explanation the laundry said it meant Arse Requires Paper.

Then Barrage Balloons had appeared all around the city, to make it difficult, it was said, for low flying enemy planes; but war did not seem to be certain until now when we were being driven to Newton Mearns.

'Now who wants to go to a house where you'll have cream in your coffee in the morning', I remember one of the well-dressed, English spoken volunteers calling in the playground where I stood with a card showing my name and address and school on my chest, my gas mask at my side and the hand of my little sister Frances in mine.

I knew the smell of coffee. I had smelt it coming from shops in the town where Charlie Logan and Charlie Birchell and I often went for walks, but I had never tasted it. As to cream, we were more accustomed to condensed milk, so it did not and could not impress me much that such houses existed. Now, however, I suddenly found Frances and I being separated and myself being whisked off in a fancy car along with a lad from my area, Joe

O'Neil, to a villa in Sandringham Avenue, in the first private car I had ever been in.

The people on whom we were billeted hadn't seen a great deal of Glasgow's pre-war depression. Their house was large, spacious and luxurious and fully equipped with two bathrooms and another toilet in the cloakroom, a private nurse to look after the old lady who was ill and a kitchen maid with a half day off a week. They were rich and happy in the knowledge that they lived in the finest country in the world and now they considered it their duty to accept this intrusion upon their comfortable world. And they fulfilled their duty with aplomb.

The old man himself looked at us twice. With the first sight he telephoned Stewart and MacDonald's in the town and instructed them to send along shoes, trousers, shirts, and a dozen pairs of top hose and some other odds and ends! The van with the clothes arrived that very afternoon to make us fit in slightly more with our new surroundings, not that we ever would completely, but it was I suppose from Mister Parker's viewpoint a step in the right direction.

The following morning I will remember all the days of my life as the first occasion on which I had ever really tasted sweet dew-stained fresh air mingled with the aromas of grass and trees and flowers.

It contrasted with the Gallowgate's foul smells from the ham curer's, the foundry and the railway. I had been on a day's trip to Cawder Woods as a boy, and the Glasgow Green was near Ross Street, so I must have smelt fresher smells than those from the L M S or Denny's before that; but I can still at a moment's notice conjure up in my mind the sensation of that air of privilege at Sandringham Avenue.

On the same morning, in a voice that wouldn't have frightened a rabbit, far less Hitler, Chamberlain made his radio announcement declaring war on Germany.

That was the second and as far as I know the last time Mister Parker looked at us. With the knowledge that the announcement about to be made was something which would alter the world about us as well as him, he called us from the avenue into the lounge which boasted plush carpets, fancy couches and French windows. We stood for the few minutes of the announcement before being ushered back out into the avenue from which Joe wandered off to look for his cousins, the Knouds, and I went in search of little Frances.

We were a bit suspicious of all this kindness and concluded that these people must be getting some kind of allowance from the Government, which of course they were, but had we stayed there the fifteen shillings or twelve and six a week did not justify our suspicions on this score or the fears we had that they were just taking us in order to grab the little message bag full of emergency rations – a couple of cans of corned beef and some biscuits – given us by the volunteers.

'What are they doing wi' oor corned mutton?' I was in the process of asking Joe while we were trying to negotiate an unobtrusive path towards the crab apple tree in the front garden, when the maid came out and asked us what we would like to have for dinner.

Such a question baffled us; we were accustomed to being told that it was herring and totties or mince or stovies for our dinner and it was strange to our ears to be asked what we would like, French beans or asparagus or . . . So after a lengthy confab which revealed that they did not know what stovies were and we had never heard of horse radish, we managed to communicate and agree on steak pie.

Ordinarily the spectacle of urchins from Glasgow's East End in the tree-lined avenues of these estates would have choked the telegraph poles with calls to the Police Office, and the appearance of so many of us to the drafting in of extra police from Giffnock or Kilmarnock, but there was patriotism in the air and by Christ these people had something to be patriotic about!

They would go on being extremely wealthy for many many years to come, but in a way we were witnessing their final fling – the end of an era. Later we would be taken to houses where we would be left in the kitchens with as many as five Highland maids catering for two or three layabouts who were perfectly capable of catering for themselves and those maids would be working, on call, for all but half a day a week, for their keep and a few miserable shillings. We would witness the actual break up of the old order occurring in another house where we were to stay, in the shape of a rather gallus, fag in the mouth, maid, who one day just buzzed off with the announcement that she was going to work in munitions.

I learned from various evacuees that there was a place called

Fingleton Mill where the stragglers among the refugees had been billeted and also that it was one hell of an uncomfortable place from which umpteen had already left for a trek back to the Gallowgate. But even there I could find no trace of Frances. It would be fully eight days before I would find that Frances, although only just eight years old, had returned home to Glasgow and to Ross Street on the same day we had been evacuated. She had just hopped on buses and trams till she got home.

On the morning of the day I got this eight days old news, I had gone along to a hall near the Mearns Cross to see a priest arrive to say Mass. He was in a most angry mood because the arrangements made for him were so inadequate. Not having as much as an Altar Boy to assist him, he picked on me for the purpose. But not knowing when the mass bell should be tinkled, or how many times it should be on such occasions, I had to sit there with a woman teacher by my side nudging me this way and that. I suppose in a way it was history in the making. It must surely have been the first Mass ever to have been offered with the assistance of an Altar Boy and an Altar Girl!

No one complimented me for my efforts but I remember proudly telling my mother when she arrived with another five of the family to visit me in Sandringham Drive that I had done my Altar Boy and I recall her being rather tickled at my question, 'How long do you have to be an Altar Boy before you become a Priest?' and gathered from her laughs that there was no necessary connection between the two vocations.

Joe and I were treated with the utmost kindness during our three months' stay in Newton Mearns and once we discovered that crab apples did not make for enjoyable eating we could not have been better behaved. Homesickness drove me home and on reflection, I wish to Christ I could have stayed.

The build-up to the war had been in little bits and pieces; slow but unsure and yet somehow sure. Ordinary folk knew little of the machinations behind the scene but they could see the sudden appearance of jobs where none had existed before; men exchanging Labour Exchange Cards which were tattered with years of vexing use for picks and shovels, sandbags appeared around public buildings; gas masks were issued to all and sundry and Glasgow Green was raised two feet to make way for an Air Raid Shelter in its bowels.

### *You heider 'im an I'll hauder 'im*

My religious belief did not prevent me breaking into shops at the age of twelve. The year was nineteen forty and there was the war and the blackout and the biggest wave of juvenile delinquency the city had ever known.

The other lads in the street had taken to shopbreaking as a new form of play and I was not going to be left out. I had to become as proficient with a jemmy as any of them. Worse still I had taken to skipping Mass and dogging school. The skipping of Mass always filled me with a guilt none of the other of our depredations caused me. I always attributed any bad luck I would have during a given week to the fact that instead of attending ten o'clock Mass in Saint Alphonsus I would be round the Barrows stealing razor blades.

When I was caught along with David Dearie and John Clarke breaking into George MacLeod's fruit store in the Candleriggs on a Sunday evening in July, I attributed my misfortune to the fact that I had failed in my duty to attend Mass that morning:

> The day will come and the day will pass
> When Orangemen will go to Mass.

When I was tried in October of that year I was sent to Saint Mary's Approved School in Bishopbriggs, there to remain for a crucial and for me painful eighteen months during which I acquired a powerful inferiority complex.

This complex was in no way eased when with puberty arrived acne, and did I have acne. My face, chest, arms and back were covered in boils and plukes at which I scrubbed and over which I poured eau-de-Cologne and Valderma all to no avail. I found jobs of a dead-end character and moved from one to the other working as a blacksmith's assistant in a foundry, as a van boy with Joseph Dunn's the lemonade people and as a message boy with Mary Fox the florist. On one occasion I was sent with a wreath to a house in Main Street, Rutherglen, and mistakenly went to houses in Main Street, Bridgeton, where I was going from door to door trying to find a taker for this wreath and no doubt frightening the lives out of a number of people who could not but have taken it as a bad omen.

With the eighteen months behind me I had given up the little game of breaking into shops but was otherwise still as daft as many other youths in the area, such as Jim Colgan.

'Come on Matt,' he said. 'Get something. We're goin' oot to fight the Stickit.' There were twenty or so others with him and each was equipped with some kind of weapon or other. I rushed off and got myself a silk stocking which I filled with stones in the back-court and was ready to join them in yet another skirmish with the Stickit, a group of lads from Queen Mary Street who were as daft as we were. Then I met John Dorans with whom I had begun palling it.

'Come on John,' says I, 'We're goin' out to fight the Stickit.'
'Oh not me Matt,' says John. 'I'm a complete coward.'
'A coward?' says I.
'A coward,' says John, 'And a very devout one too. It's my religion.'
I had never dreamed there were such things. If someone dared you, you did. It was the culture of the Calton.

That culture had already destroyed and would destroy many men, men like its then Best Fighter, Algy Airnes.

Algy's half brother Finnie Young had played football for many Junior and Senior teams and had in fact been signed on for Celtic when he was whisked off to fight in the Second World War in which he was killed.

Everyone, including Finnie himself and every expert in football in the area, and there were no shortages of such experts, agreed that Algie was a far better player than Finnie. He had the best left foot in the business. But he was too strong physically. Not for football, but for the Calton.

If you were strong you fought, even if it were only in defence of others and if you were a winner you were then a challenge to every up-and-coming fighter.

Algie Airnes, the leader of the Ross Street lads, after having spent the bulk of his life behind bars, died in his early fifties, a spent and wasted man. It was a culture which had destroyed men like Tam the Hawk and Scout O'Neil. Big Scout was so called because whenever there was a Clabber or back-court concert in the Ham Pend he would sing the Dave Willis song:

When I was young my mother told me always to be good
And do the best I could for everyone.
So I've taken her advice I've joined the gallant scouts
I joined because I felt just in the mood.
My duty is to do a good deed almost every day
And as I go along the road you'll always hear me say

*For I'm a scout scout scout and you'll always hear me shout*
*Paloo paloo paloo it's my patrol*
*I shout about about about just to try and find things out*
*I'm as good as a bloodhound wi' my hat and pole*

But Scout did not do much singing when Tam the Hawk was around for they indeed fought and fought and fought and ran between them a thirty year feud. With razors and bayonets they had fought in youth and then had kept the fight going into old age and were over the fifty mark when Tam the Hawk was shot in the buttock through the door of his house in the Hawkhead building in the Gallowgate.

For years Tam drank in a pub in Kent Street, always with his back to the wall and with a wary eye open in case his rival would appear. The Scout for his part had always to keep his eyes peeled for The Hawk.

What a culture, what a drag down of human dignity. In the Calton culture the fighting men were the heroes. The highest hope of a boy in that culture was to become such an idiot. The biggest insult you could be given was for someone to say they could fight you.

On leaving the Approved School I was told to report once a month to the school authorities and give an account of myself. One Sunday while there on such a mission a boy approached me.

'Do you know Jimmy Quinn?'

'Aye,' says I.

'He says he gave you a doing,' says the boy.

Jimmy, now an inmate of the school, was out for the day, it being Sunday and he being of good behaviour and having done seven months of his time. I knew that he would be coming off the tram at Bishopbriggs terminus just after four o'clock which was in three hours' time. I rushed down to the terminus to wait the three hours for poor Jimmy who came off the tram to have this idiot challenging him in a temper that would have started a fight in a monastery.

'Did you tell people you could fight me?' Naw Matt, naw I didnae,' says Jimmy, restoring to me a certain peace of mind. Well, I mean you just can't have people going around the world saying they can fight you. It could well spread. You could have them going around Hong Kong saying, 'I can fight Matt McGinn.' And you could have other people believing them. Think of your reputation.

There were lots of good and reasonable, respectable people in the area but for others the place was a litter bin filled with scarred faces and minds and prison records the length of your arm. It was a culture which did not allow cowards. I had never dreamed there were such things until then, but suddenly realised that in regards to idiotic things, like fighting the Stickit, I too was a coward and threw away the weapon and decided that Jim and his pals could manage in their stupid behaviour without me.

I had never until then seriously questioned the culture of the Calton nor the cultures of society in general. But around this time John and Tommy Alston and I stumbled upon Brunswick Street, which was then Glasgow's equivalent of Hyde Park corner. We had been on our way to a dance hall in Dundas Street when, with a little time on hand we stopped to listen to some of the Socialists, Anarchists and atheists like Sam Bryden, a blacksmith from the Blythswood shipyard. This was my first university.

## Change the Scheme of Things

A slightly older lad from Ross Street, Robert Lynn, was then with the Anarchists and he set to work on us with his idea of a different kind of society, for which I fell hook line and sinker. It was a dream world and I caught hold of the dream, a Utopia where there would be no jails and no police because there would be no crime and no money.

'But what about people stealing?' says I. 'Nobody would steal,' says Robert, 'because it would be a society of abundance. What would be the sense in stealing in such a society? Let's take as an example the most precious material things to man. What would you say these were?' Air,' says I, 'and water.' 'Exactly,' says Robert, 'and these are in abundance. Now how would you like to steal some air and some water and go round the Gallowgate trying to sell it. Now if we can create a society where everything else is in

B

abundance and we can do that, with modern technology, stealing would vanish.'

I was bitten by the political bug and I followed Robert's direction and got from the Bridgeton and Stirling's Libraries *The Rights of Man* by Tom Paine, and a very heavy-going book, *Das Kapital*, by a man called Karl Marx. I had a good look at the Bible and found a great many contradictions there. I read Secular Society tracts and political pamphlets about such subjects as Dialectical and Historical Materialism. I got a dictionary and learned an entirely new vocabulary building it up three, four and five words a day. Soon I was standing on my own soap box in Brunswick Street roaring and bawling. I had entered a fascinating world where I would be led hither and thither.

I joined the Communist Party in nineteen forty nine. And boy was I a believer. Marxism was to me like a new religion through which we would create a paradise on earth. Everything has within it the seed of its own destruction including Capitalism, its seed being the proletariat which it inevitably brought into being. This class would do battle with the bourgeoisie and usher in a classless society of abundance.

Round the pubs I went with the *Daily Worker*, often even giving them away to the boozers gathered there. Down on the streets I went with the chalk and the whitewash, up on the platform I went with my stentorian voice roaring and bawling, in Brunswick Street and at the Barrows. The revolution was round the corner, imperialism was collapsing throughout the world and The Party would lead the working class into glory. Join The Party!

I recruited them by the dozen, got special mention in the Party's magazines and was brought on to platforms and congratulated as a top recruiter. I wrote letters to the papers challenging the anti-communists who dared to suggest that there were prison camps in the Soviet Union. 'Name the camps,' I challenged and when they did I dismissed them as liars. The Party was the perfect instrument.

### Ru'glen Jean

I have a natural and profound respect for women, to whom I have also unfortunately always felt inferior. My mother, I suppose, is in part responsible for this, being as she was a complete giver, a non-taker so far as her family were concerned. Twenty-four hours a day she was there for us and I don't think she ever entertained in her mind an inkling of a notion unconnected with her children.

In addition she was always a good worker on behalf of and a friend towards all of those in our small and large community in the Calton district. No-one ever came to her in need of help and went away empty-handed. She would run miles for people and always find her own solution for the smaller problems with which people were confronted, whether it was a rent default or a confinement where the mother-to-be could not afford the half crown for the midwife or someone who could not pay a fine or where there was a body to wash, or a 'Sheet' to be gone round with for funeral expenses. Nelly Havlin McGinn was never found wanting.

There were also my sisters Dinah, Nelly, Lizzie, Patricia and Frances who always showered love upon me with a loyalty unbending.

Only recently a New York disc jockey, a so-called expert on Folk Music, Oscar Brand, had a sample of this when during a phone-in on a radio programme he runs in that city he was asked by a caller why Matt McGinn was not 'bigger' in the field and had replied with some derogatory remarks about myself, which might well have been justified. I have been spared the knowledge of what the remarks were, so I wouldn't know.

Apparently two callers phoned in my defence, the first of these was my sister Pat, a New Yorker for twenty years and she was yelling at Brand over the phone, 'Hey, that's my brother you're talking about!'

Then too there was my wife, Janette. She walked into the small room of the Bridgeton Public Hall and took a seat in front of us among the twenty or so Communist Party members, Young Communist Leaguers and fellow travellers there assembled to hear Bill Joss speak on the forthcoming election.

'Big Smasher' said John Dorans to me. 'A fine big animal,' said I, having taken in the picture of a tall, slim, well-proportioned lovely with thick rich flaxen blonde hair cut short, a sweet Alice Faye type face and although just eighteen years old she had a ladylike and sedate bearing. It was the first time I had seen Janette and I little dreamed that in a few months time she and I would be preparing our little 'single end' in the Little Dovehill off the Gallowgate. She was, someone said, Janette Gallacher and would be working as the secretary in headquarters of the Bridgeton Party set in a shop in the broken-down and overcrowded Nuneaton Street in Dalmarnock, which shop had been specially rented for the election. It was a month before I saw her again in those headquarters.

As I entered there was a row raging in the shop between a Comrade, John McIvor, and Ned McDonald with whom he had been canvassing in a nearby close. McIvor claimed that McDonald had 'engaged in and conducted himself in an unseemly and non-Communist manner towards a fellow member of the exploited classes'. They had gone to a door, one of three on the third landing, and their knock had been answered by a wee poorly-dressed four year old. 'Daddy, it's two MANS,' the wee girl had thrown back into the kitchen. 'Tell them tae come in,' came a hoarse voice from the kitchen whence also came the smells of decayed masonry, dampness and cabbage, the latter from a pot on the half range above which hung a picture of King Billy crossing the Boyne, with the wallpaper peeling around it. The possessor of the hoarse voice sat dressed in a jacket, bonnet and red, white and blue scarf, his bared feet stuck in a zinc basin of soapy water.

'What dae ye want?' he asked.

'We're here,' said McIvor, 'to canvass on behalf of Dan Kelly.'

'Kelly,' said the man. 'Another Pape eh?'

'Naw,' says McIvor. 'Communist.'

'Communist,' the man exploded, now standing up in the basin into which his trouser legs fell. 'The cause of a' the trouble in this country. If I'd my way I'd hang the lot of ye. And for a start I'll throw the two of you down that fucking stair. I'm a true blue Tory.'

At this McDonald, a building trade worker, had hit the man with a bundle of leaflets and shouted, 'Tory! Living in a place like this. It's yer fucking heid you should be steeping in that basin!'

'It was disgraceful,' McIvor was saying, 'I'm going to report you to the Glasgow Committee.'

Between Janette and me there was an immediate rapport but I still had no dream that a fine girl like this would have anything to do with a Gallowgate corner boy like me.

A few nights later after a coffee in a nearby cafe where there was a nickelodeon which seemed to play nothing but the nickelodeon song, 'Put Another Nickel In', I escorted her on a tram to Rutherglen from the main part of which her mother and father had just moved to a house in Spittal near Cathkin Braes. She had a good mile's walk up a darkened road from the tram stop and I was flattered when she asked me to accompany her.

'I think I'm entitled to a reward for that,' said I under the bridge at the top. She agreed and we kissed under the light. From then on we were together as often as could be whether in the Cosmo Cinema or selling the Y.C.L. paper *Challenge* or the *Daily Worker* or whitewashing the streets with political slogans or painting revolutionary slogans like, 'Cut the Call Up' on the walls of the Army Recruiting office in Dalmarnock Road or merely walking in Cathkin.

The first time I took her to my mother's home in Ross Street I asked her if she fancied getting married and to my astonishment she agreed. My mother always had a good name with Faulds the Factor in Risk Street and she was able with ease to get us the little one-roomed house in Little Dovehill. It was above the room and kitchen she had gotten for my sister Lizzie and her man Tommy Reilly. We had the house a month before we were married which gave us time to have the place papered and painted.

Here there was a slight clash, I with my taste in the soles of my feet suggesting pink and Janette white! White! I had never heard of such a thing but I gave way and set to on the existing dark brown of the woodwork. When I had it painted it looked ghastly, the dark brown still streaking through. 'The proof of the pudding . . .' says I and rushed down to Clyde Books, then in Anderston, where Janette was then working and where I found her looking extremely attractive. She remained, in spite of my panic, cool as she normally did in a crisis.

'Did you think of putting on another coat?' said Janette.

'Another coat!' says I. 'Just wait till you see it!' We did together put on another two coats and the effect was overall beautiful.

I was then working in a whisky bond and with selling the 'carry out' of a bottle of undiluted and young whisky a day, a practice in which I and every other worker in the place engaged to supplement the miserly wages, I had managed to gather together forty pounds in the Post Office savings bank; with this I intended to buy a really good wedding ring.

When I suggested this to Janette she 'pooh hooed' the idea. 'We need a new bed and some second-hand furniture before we think of a ring.' Janette's mother bought us a new bed and we visited Johnny Wilson's second-hand furniture store to secure a second-hand dining room suite. This we had delivered that day, my having paid the forty quid cash. The little house was like a palace by the time she had it finished.

'But what about the ring?' says I.

'I'll get one at Woolworth's,' she said coolly.

'You cannae dae that, that would be ridiculous,' says I.

'You can get me a proper one when we can afford it,' says Janette and that was that.

> For Christmas he bought her a wee golden ring
> But later it made him embarrassed
> He'd forgot the first thing to turn green in the Spring
> Was jewellery bought at the barras

We were married in the Registrar's Office with my placing her mother's ring upon her finger, with Janette's sister Ann her best maid and she dressed in matching and beautiful powdered turquoise suits and with my pal, John Dorans, the best man, lending me seven and six to pay for the licence. For six months Janette wore the Woolworth's ring with which she had replaced her mother's when we got back from the reception in her parents' home in Mossgeil Avenue in Rutherglen. It was to be a turbulent marriage but during the time in Little Dovehill we did have many happy happy hours.

Apart from the fact that the Gallowgate was then deteriorating rapidly Janette was anxious to move to Rutherglen, near her mother, and so six months after our first daughter Anna was born we moved to Fifty Eight High Street in the ancient burgh of Rutherglen. It was altogether a better area in which to bring up children but the house, another single end, was even smaller than the box we had left in Little Dovehill. It was made even smaller, shortly afterwards, by the arrival of our son Matt.

It was six years later before we got our first decent house, a new three apartment in Fernhill with a bathroom and kitchen and back and front gardens. It was like arriving in paradise and for two days I became a keen gardener, as did Matt. Then a small boy, he was out on the first day killing worms. 'Don't dae that son,' says I. 'Worms are good for the soil. They make wee holes in it and let the air and the water in and help things to grow.' Next day Matt and

With Janette, on hiking holiday, 1951.

some of his new-found pals like Rab Knape and Ian Kirk were down in the nearby field busily at work on a programme which the genius of a boy had logically worked out from my horticultural lecture and after a few hours they came up with three shovels full of red wriggling creatures which they deposited in our front garden.

'That's some worms to help the garden Dad', said Matt proudly!

While in Fernhill we had another two children, Eleanor and Shonagh, following which we had to apply for a bigger house from the Scottish Special Housing Association; from them we obtained a four apartment in Spittal.

### I never did like being idle

In Harland and Wolff's in Finnieston I was enjoying my job as a storeman. Among other things it was intriguing to find how many things the mind can take in. There were a quarter of a million items there stored and it astonished me that within a month of starting work you could pick up an order sheet at the desk from the engineering workers who wanted liners of screws or bolts, and within a couple of minutes you could have found the item from among all those and have it in the hands of the worker wanting it.

But I wasn't destined to spend a lifetime there. The gaffer did not like it when I made an attempt to get the storemen into a Union, as all the tradesmen were.

I was not the only one the gaffer did not savour. There was a harrier there called John who would have made it impossible for any gaffer to like any other worker grafting alongside him. Besides John all of us others were like tortoises. He ran from Shettleston, of whose Harriers he was a member, to Finnieston, a distance of some five miles every morning. He ran from Finnieston to Shettleston at night when he had finished work even on overtime nights and he ran all day at his work.

So anyway I would have gone, but the gaffer did not want to say anything direct about the Union organising. He waited till I was up a ladder outside his despatch office where I was singing 'Old Man River That Old Man River He must know something but he don't say nothing.' The he came rushing out, a round-figured man in brown dungarees and similar coloured hat.

'Cut out that singing,' he bawled.

'Why should I stop singing,' says I. 'I'm happy.'

'You're happy,' he says. 'You're sacked. And I'll have you blacklisted throughout the Clyde.'

'For singing?' says I.

'Aye,' says he. 'A lot of fucking Darky songs.'

Come to think of it, Harland's and me were never designed to be friends. Six months I was with them in their Govan yard and we didn't get on well together.

The charisma wasn't there in my relationship with their head timekeeper, for example, who one day walked into the platers' shed and kicked over the brazier fire sending burning coals sprawling at the feet of the men. A nice chap he was and it was just his wee way of showing his slight disapproval of the men having been boiling their cans a few minutes before dinner time. It was a pity mind you that it left some of the men without tea for their 'lunch' but these things happen. After trying unsuccessfully to get some of the men nonetheless to complain that it wasn't precisely the way they liked to be treated I decided to go it alone. Well not exactly alone. I was after all the 'Burners' Helpers' Shop Steward'. (How low can you get?)

'I would like to see the head timekeeper please,' I spoke to one of his aides. 'And who are you?' said he without looking up from the desk where he was scanning over some papers. 'My name is McGinn. I am the Burners' Helpers' Shop Steward N U G M W.' 'Oh,' he said, most impressed. 'And what do you want to see him about?' 'Well,' says I. 'He's after kicking over a fire in the platers' shed, to which I cannot object, although I should imagine your insurance company might, but the men's tea and sugar and cans were kicked over in the process and I want to demand an apology; either that or police proceedings are going to be taken on the grounds that he was thereby interfering with the men's private property.' 'Aye well,' said he staring smirkily into my face, 'I'll leave word to that effect.'

It was now well into the dinner break and there was a meeting about to be held outside the gate at which I was due to speak and when I did get up I was ranting on about the management having taken up the game of 'Kick the Can' and generally lambasting this Napoleonic attitude of a haughty and dangerous twit.

At precisely three o'clock that day Sammy Wylie the burner and I were heating up our cans for tea, when a bowler hat popped up from the side of the boat and a voice quietly said, 'Up you two go to the office and collect your cards.' Quietly we went and did collect. The money and cards were lying waiting and made up to the penny. As we were walking out of the office, another bowler pulled Sam aside, 'Hold on a second, Mister Wylie.'

I waited outside for Sam who came out with a disturbed look on his face. 'They've asked me to start in the morning,' said Sammy. 'I'm no' gonnie dae that.' 'Look Sam for Christ sake, they're out to get me and they'll have done it one way or another. Just you start in the morning.'

Around this period I worked in another Clyde shipyard which shall remain un-named in case Sir Eric Yarrow gets angry but there I was in the lofty and mind-boggling position of a Plumber's Helper and would you believe it held the post of Plumbers' Helpers' Shop Steward. I'll get to the top of the Trade Union movement yet.

Nothing very exciting happened there except that this time I did not feel so terribly alone when the time came to part company with Yarrows. There were seven members of the Communist Party in the plumbers' shop who were all active selling the *Daily Worker* of a morning and what not and one day the Management pounced and sacked the seven of us, throwing in five Catholics for good measure and so no one could possibly accuse them of discrimination.

### Lots of Little Soldiers

In nineteen fifty two came this Gorbals Branch business and to my mind a blatant contradiction appeared in the picture I had of the Communist Party. Harry McShane and Andy McLeary and the other members of the Gorbals Branch Committee had passed a resolution alleging that the Glasgow Secretary Bob McIlhone was adopting a Napoleonic attitude to members and that too little was being done to develop opposition to the War in Korea then raging. They had called for an enquiry into the Glasgow leadership.

Instead of this the Glasgow Committee decided to enquire into the Gorbals Branch and suspended McShane, McLeary and the others from their positions in that Branch. But here came the contradiction to me and a few others in the Bridgeton Branch of which I was a member.

Harry McShane was *Daily Worker* reporter and also a member of the Scottish Committee, and my reasoning was that if Harry was still fit to remain executive in these positions he was surely fit to remain as a member of the Gorbals Executive. I began to voice criticisms of this and of the fact that monthly aggregate meetings of the Glasgow membership were not being held.

Janette and I had moved to High Street in Rutherglen and in this abode one of our first visitors was a Comrade from the Rutherglen Branch ostensibly to invite us to join his Branch. This invitation I declined on the grounds that my roots were in Bridgeton and I wished to remain in that Branch where I thought I could be more effective. His real motive however soon came to light when he provoked me into uttering my criticism of the leadership.

Returning from work one evening I found that there was a telegram ordering me to appear before the Scottish Executive in Miller Street. 'Ha Ha,' says I. 'At last they're recognising my talents and they're going to offer me a position as a full-time revolutionary' and off I went to appear before the Vanguard of the Scottish Proletariat.

At Miller Street I found I was not alone in having been telegrammed. Hugh Savage, Andy McLeary, Ned Donaldson and Les Forster were also there and we were there to be carpeted like naughty little boys. All of my criticisms to the Rutherglen member were repeated.

'You know, Comrades, that factions will not be tolerated in The Party,' a bald-headed man boomed, his finger pointing at one of us and then another. 'We are not saying that you have a faction functioning, but there are certain signs,' the bald man said ominously and proceeded to list his evidence.

'Comrade McGinn for example was heard criticising the leadership and even Harry Pollit, the General Secretary, and you know that when you criticise the leadership here you are criticising the Soviet Party and Comrade Stalin himself, and Comrade Mao Tse Tung as well.' The mere utterance of these words made the bald-headed man's companions grit their teeth! 'Comrade McGinn was seen at the interval of the recent Scottish Congress in the Woodside Halls going into a cafe in Maryhill Road with Comrade McShane.' It was a childish affair, but had these people been in power you can put the pot on for it that little old me would not have lived to write those words, and the five of us would have joined thousands of others like Lansky in Czechoslovakia in being executed, perhaps to be rehabilitated and reburied at a later date as were so many following Kruschev's speech at the Twentieth Congress of the Soviet Communist Party in nineteen fifty six.

Les Forster and Ned Donaldson were suspended and in protest Harry McShane, Hugh Savage and I resigned, Harry giving his story to the *News Chronicle*. This latter act was the crime of the century, 'See, the lackey went off to the bourgeois press.'

I heard that there was to be an aggregate meeting and as the lack of these meetings was one of my main criticisms, I rejoined. The meeting was a comic opera affair which was designed to prepare a press statement, yes, for the bourgeois press.

'What is this about a spy being sent into Comrade McGinn's house,' someone asked. 'There never was a spy,' said Comrade Lauchlin, the Scottish Secretary, and my wife Janette who was eight months pregnant with Matt, walked over to the other side of the hall and stood beside the Rutherglen man who had come into my house. 'Here is the spy,' Janette shouted. 'My mother and I asked him why he had rushed up to the Scottish leadership and repeated everything said in our house and he said, "I was sent to your house. The Scottish leadership were convinced there was a faction functioning, that McShane was a member of it and that McGinn was a weak link in the chain and would talk."'

The Rutherglen man sat like a sheep without a Bah and Janette rushed towards the platform with accusations and counter-accusations being shouted from every part of the hall. I was afraid for the baby Janette was carrying and rushed after her to pull her back.

Suddenly amid the great babble and hubbub the bald-headed man who was chairing the meeting rose and said in a sad voice, 'Comrades, we are sorry to have to announce that Comrade Willie MacFarlane of the Partick Branch died three days ago and I'd like you to be upstanding for two minutes silence.'

'Come on Janette,' says I. 'They're looking for a press statement.' Then I tore up my card and threw the pieces on the floor of the hall. I still did not know what was basically wrong and a few months later rejoined, finally leaving in Easter nineteen fifty six after I had initiated the first debate which had been allowed at the British Congress of the Communist Party since nineteen forty one.

My motion was against the Party's support of conscription, and was defeated, so that the Communist Party became the last political party in Britain to support conscription even after the Tories had abolished it. After its being abolished by the Tories, the best the advance guard of the proletariat could do was to have the Young Communist League pass a resolution that the League should oppose any return to conscription.

## *If it wisnae for the Union*

I got a job in the noisiest factory in Britain, Guest Keen and Nettlefold's in Hillington, where they produced woodscrews, or screwnails. Huge rolls of steel wire of all gauges were brought in at one end of the rectangular building to be put through heading machines where they were cut and hammered to create the head, through turning machines where they were trimmed and sawcut, and through 'worming' machines where they were given their twisted stems all to a great clatter bang, thud and wallop of steel upon iron and iron upon concrete which made every bone in your body shake.

The sound was so great that occasionally a worker sent there by the Labour Exchange would simply turn and walk out the door the minute he had entered. But many of us, myself included, were too glad of the job to worry about the noise and it was with some satisfaction that I got myself employed there as a Machine Operator working shifts.

But I was only there two days when I was in the wars. The Shops Stewards Convener, Paddy O'Hare, was co-operating with the Management in introducing a new Time and Study scheme which consisted of increasing the work load by one third in return for a ten percent increase in wages and there was a meeting arranged in the canteen on my second day in the factory which would be addressed by the Manager, Mr Cox, and by Paddy O'Hare who was in the Chair.

It was a cakewalk for the Management and I could not hold my tongue. 'Brother Chairman,' says I. 'I started here yesterday because I was sacked along with all the other workers in a Bird Cage Factory. We were sacked because they introduced a scheme similar to this and we finished up making so many bird cages there wasnae any room in the building for us.'

Next day I was taken off the machines and put on the dayshift to be ready for the bullet out the door.

Big Frank Reid who came from the Gallowgate was among the

dayshift workers who had all left the Union because it was doing nothing for them and he got to work.

'We're all going back into the Union and we're gonnie make you the dayshift Shop Steward,' Frank said to me. Paddy O'Hare got wind of this and later told me that he had gone to the manager who was intent on sacking me, and said to Cox, 'Put him back on the machines on my shift and I'll see that he doesnae cause any trouble.' In any case there was still the possibility that I would fail in the three week training period to become efficient enough at the machine and this indeed was a possibility as I had never handled anything mechanical in my life. But here they would be thwarted by young Alex Thomson, a skilled fitter who took a liking to me and set to work specially training me for the job so that there would be no question of my failing.

Paddy had been doing a poor job of his shop stewardship so that a number of minor and major grievances were accumulating among the men who felt among other things that they were being cheated of their bonuses. One of the foremen, who were all Englishmen, this being a colonial outpost from their main Birmingham plant, came round one night with the tally sheets. These tallies showed or purported to show how much each machine had produced the previous day. On this particular evening they were especially low, causing great discontent.

What we would find out later was that there was a hole in one of the cleaning plants through which the screwnails were falling, but at this moment there was just a sense that we were being cheated and I went round all the machine operators in the turning section: 'Are you prepared to put off your machines if everyone else is?' 'Aye well if . . . .' was the reply of a few. But enough of us were strong on it and I jammed off my machine to be followed by Alex Thomson and Ronnie Summerfield and all the others in the turning section.

The sudden diminution of noise brought Jimmy Pann running from the worming section.

'What is it, Matt?'

'Strike,' says I and Jimmy rushed over and started putting off the worming machines. Jimmy McKinnon came over from the heading section and did similarly with those machines.

The place had been in operation for twelve years and there had never been any action of this sort so it was a slightly baffled

46

foreman who bobbed up his bespectacled head from the foremen's 'look-out' as I took a group of the men over to Paddy O'Hare who was still working at the cleaning plant. 'Right,' I shouted at Paddy. 'We've stuck off the machines and they're not going on again till we get the question of the tallies sorted out.' Paddy looked round the faces of the men, bit his lip, stuck his fingers in his waistcoat pocket and said, 'Right, Canteen!'

In the canteen I put the case for a strike, a case which was seconded by Alex Thomson. 'We'll vote on it,' said Paddy. 'Now is there anyone against?' he asked. A wall of silence greeted his question. 'Now,' says Paddy, correctly, 'Strike action is a serious business and I don't want anybody voting for a strike and then the minute they're out that door talking against it.' Three times Paddy repeated this warning and then took the vote which · was unanimous.

As we left the canteen a little old man, who had just stuck his hand up for the strike, was shaking his head, 'I don't see whit good strikes dae,' he was muttering, reminding me of John S. Clarke's 'Farewell to the Working Class':

> There is a thing that lacks a spine
> In every shipyard, mill and mine.

The strike lasted a couple of days with a list of grievances having been thrashed out and settled.

I was elected Shop Steward and remained in the factory for four and a half years, to leave for Oxford having won a Transport and General Workers Union scholarship to Ruskin College.

The scholarship I had won largely on the basis of an essay I had submitted:

'Nothing is more surprising than the ease with which the few govern the many'. Discuss.

In the two thousand words required I argued that there was nothing surprising about it, that we are conditioned from birth by parents, by teachers, preachers, policemen, foremen and employers to be easily ruled and thereby won the privilege of Ruskin, the best college in Britain, for two years.

In that two years I studied for the Oxford University Diploma in Economics and Political Science and enjoyed every minute of it. The place was scintillating with ideas and knowledge, a great deal

Nuffield College, Oxford, 1957.

of which I imbibed. By comparison, Huddersfield Teachers Training College to which I went for the following year to obtain the Leeds University Certificate in Education was dull. But it was while at Huddersfield that I made the move that was to take me into the 'Folk' music field.

### They hang me the morra for pullin the plug

I was to enter it through a competition, one of three run by the then *Reynold's News* (later to become the *Sunday Citizen*). While at Huddersfield I read of the three competitions, one for a television play, one for a short story and the third for a song 'in the folk song tradition'.

48

'Right,' says I. 'This is for me. Am I not the man to win all three competitions, don't I badly need the money, isn't Janette waiting up there in Bonnie Rutherglen for me to bring home such prizes, won't my children be proud to see their Pop's name in the paper as the winner?' Paul Zammit, my Maltese pal was with me and I said 'Paul, I'm going to win all three of these, just you leave me for a day or two and I'll show you.'

Into the library I went with a pile of paper and a pen and two days afterwards I emerged with a short story, a television play and a song 'The Foreman O'Rourke', about a man who had murdered his gaffer in a shipyard lavatory by pulling the plug on his head and who was about to be hanged for his misdeed in Barlinnie Prison. 'You're a genius McGinn,' said Paul, his brown eyes bulging with admiration. 'Of course I am,' says I. 'And have I not always told you so?' 'Indeed you have,' said Paul. 'On many occasions.'

I stuck the song along with another couple of ditties on a tape and with those and the manuscripts off we went to the post box and the pub where Paul and I got drunk on beer and conversation.

'I told the Prime Minister Mintoff,' said Paul, 'all about this great Scotsman Matt McGinn. I sat into the wee small hours of the morning with him telling him about you and I am sure that if you want a teaching job in Malta when you finish up here he will fix you up.'

That was a nice thought but I had other intentions when I left Huddersfield. I was going to earn my bread by the pen, and wasn't I going to win this competition? 'Certainly you are,' said Paul and I bought him another pint.

Two Thursdays after this a dark-haired bespectacled man appeared at the hostel with a camera in his hand and a request to see me on his tongue.

'I'm a freelance journalist and I have been asked to take a picture of you for *Reynold's News*,' said he causing my heart to miss a couple of beats. 'Have I won?' says I. 'I can't tell you,' said Specky. 'What have I won, is it the song, the play, the story?' said I. Clicking his camera he ignored my pleas. 'Look, for God's sake, man, give us a hint,' I begged. 'I can't tell you,' says he and off he went to leave me without sleep for the next three nights.

On the Sunday morning I was up with the first streaks of daylight and off to the Huddersfield Railway Station, where I waited for three hours for the newsvendor to arrive with his bundles and with a suspicious look on his swarthy face – apparently he thought I was waiting there to roll him. '*Reynold's News*,' says I, and it was clear from the little hunchback's eyes that the Scottish accent in no way allayed his fears. He cut the string around a bundle of papers and almost threatened me with the knife as he took the coppers in exchange for the precious paper which I feverishly opened, to find to my joy that there was the headline 'Song Winner', above a picture of me.

The TV play and the story had gone on the bing but the song had won first prize. The judges, Peggy Seeger, Bert Lloyd and Charles Parker of the BBC were unanimous in their choice of first prize, 'The Foreman O'Rourke'. But I was to find out later that the editor was equally adamant that it was not to be. He sent for the three judges. 'Pick me another winner,' he instructed them. 'I can't publish that.' 'No. That is the winner,' said Peggy, Bert and Charles and stuck to their guns.

'Give me all your *Reynold's News*,' I yelled and by now the little vendor was obviously convinced he was dealing with some kind of madman, who walked about the streets of English cities all night and then in the morning attacked little hunchbacked newsvendors.

'Eh?' he muttered, his face whitening. 'What?'

I held out a pound note which seemed to settle him a little. 'Give me all of your *Reynold News*,' says I, adding to myself 'and ask me why, ya little nyaff.' But if he was interested in why it didn't show. I wandered back to college gloating over my newspapers.

That was a week before I left and I was sure that now within hours or days at least the whole music publishing world would be descending upon this new songwriter phenomenon which had just shattered his way into their world. But no. Things don't happen that way for me. And most assuredly not with songs like 'The Foreman O'Rourke'.

No-one jumped at the song or at me.

It reminds me a little of the story of the composer who took a manuscript around Tin Pan Alley where all of the publishers agreed it was the most beautiful piece of music they had ever heard, but equally unanimously refused to do anything with it on the flimsy excuse that he refused them permission to alter the title from, 'I Love You So Much, You Make Me Want The Lavatory'. But I thought I was no small drink as I made my way home to Glasgow with my diploma, certificate and newsclipping.

With friends at Ruskin, 1959. 'Mambo' Macoco 3rd from left.

### *You cannae spend a dollar when you're deid*

Back in Glasgow the Anti-Polaris Base movement was in full swing with regular demonstrations at the Holy Loch in Dunoon, with trade unionists, left-wingers and Nationalists being arrested for sitting down in front of the Base gates and such offences, and leading this movement was a one-man folk revival called Josh McRae. Josh was the nearest thing to a pop idol that the revival in Scotland had produced. A dark and handsome man often accused of being a physical reincarnation of Rabbie Burns, Josh was an Art teacher in Adelphi Street School who had fallen in love with the songs of the American black singer Josh White and in particular those songs of White's that made social and political comment. So Josh had taught himself guitar, learned a few hundred songs and proceeded to set the Clyde alight. Norman Buchan and his wife Janey gave him a hand to form a group with a brother of Janey's and two girls from Clydebank, the Swankie Sisters. The group was known as the Rievers which after some good recording and TV work broke up leaving Josh on his own to lead off the 'Glasgow Eskimoes' a loose grouping of singers whose concentration was upon getting that Base out of the Clyde.

With Josh McRae, early 1960s.

'Och Och Get oot the Holy Loch', and 'Ye Cannae Spend a Dollar When yer Deid' – his voice could be heard ringing throughout the country on television (in which medium he was in the process of sacrificing a promising lucrative career by his singing of anti-establishment songs, about Polaris and the Royal Family as well):

> Noo Scotland hasnae got a king and she hasnae got a queen
> For ye canne hae the second Liz whaur the first yin's never been

Why couldn't he have stuck to those old songs which were on ancient battles now safe to talk or sing about? But no, he would insist on firing from his guitar and larynx the bullets being forged by the pens of folk like Thurso Berwick and Jim MacLean:

> Wee Prince Charlie's a lucky laddie
> He's got a Mammy and a Daddy

As an outlet for contemporary song the Eskimoes had given and were giving stimulus to the creation of hundreds of songs. So, while Hamish Henderson was penning 'Freedom Come All Ye', school teacher Adam McNaughtan, who would later send his Starvation Height song, 'Ye cannae fling pieces oot a twenty storey flat', spinning around the world, was busy writing parodies and I was very much on the fringe of all this. But I was busy. My first task was to find myself a job, but a difficulty here was that my teaching qualifications were English and if I were to get a proper teaching job it would have to be in the land where I had qualified. I made applications to various colleges and while I waited, relying on Janette's wages, I wrote songs with a prolificacy which astonished even myself. I had found or was sure I was about to find an outlet for things that were in my mind and I was getting ready to be in with the horns down. I read in the papers about a family who had moved out of a house in Govan because they claimed there was a ghost in it. With my kids around me I poured out The Dundee Ghost.

> Noo a deid man seldom walks and he very rarely talks
> It's no' very often you'll find him running aroon
> But I am a refugee fae a graveyard in Dundee
> And I've come to haunt some hooses in Glesga Toon, etc.

And I wrote hundreds of others.


## Where have all the flowers gone?

The most beautiful red rose in the world is a weed if it finds itself flourishing in a cultivated cabbage patch. But Norrie Buchan was a cultivator of neither cabbages nor roses and if they chose to grow side by side in the big jungle-like and rambling garden of his house in Peel Street, Partick, who was he to consider them weeds or to interfere with this manner of bragging and boasting of nature.

'Don't look,' he muttered with the slightest hint of an apology as he led me along the path to the back of the huge house, the upper part of which he and Janey had recently acquired, the lower part of it having been taken over by other friends of ours, Andy McLeary and his wife.

Of lean build, Norrie, who would later become a government Minister, was a dynamo, whose build denied the fact that he had been a university boxing champion and that he was an eighteen-hour-a-day teacher, politician, poet and organiser of folk song clubs, groups and concerts. It was in the organisation of a concert in the Saint Andrew's Halls in Glasgow that he was primarily interested at this moment.

Pete Seeger was on a tour of Britain and Norrie and Janey were taking care of the Scottish side of it.

Norrie was from the North East of Scotland, a place rich in songs of people and that coupled with his interest in and teaching of literature had led him to a love of the ballads, to the formation of a Ballads Club in Rutherglen Academy, and perchance into the promotion of their singing by people like Josh McRae.

Norrie had had considerable successes in organising concerts for Josh and was now bringing his experience to bear for the organisation of this one for Pete. And before leaving London Pete had asked Norrie to arrange for him to meet me while he was in Scotland.

In the Buchans' kitchen Pete, at six foot three, towered over me and shook hands. 'Gosh, you know I've been wanting to meet you since Ewan MacColl played me a tape of some of your songs in London. I only wish that I could write a song that is worth

54

repeating and you have written so many. I want to hear some more.'

The guy was so modest and yet so patently honest that I was just able to clip my tongue on the question, 'Who are you kidding?'

Here was the man who had written, 'Where Have all the Flowers Gone' which was creating a sensation wherever it was sung and who had had many other fine songs in the charts of many countries, talking to a little Glasgow man who was struggling to make ends meet with no such success or fame to his credit. The modesty of this wonderful man who had become a legend haunting the conscience of America with his love of and his rendition of the songs of his native land and of the world and who had become a thorn in the flesh of the House of Un-American Activities Committee in Washington, overwhelmed me.

A beautiful, Eurasian-blooded, all-American woman entered and was introduced as Pete's wife Toshi. She was his protector. A noble woman with that certain toughness that only American women seem to be able to acquire, Toshi knew what the world was about and you could immediately understand that here was a shield to this giant of a man who had just been sentenced to one year's imprisonment by the aforementioned Un-American Committee, against which sentence he was currently appealing.

We were discussing songs and the revival when an urgent phone call came through from my wife Janette informing me that I had come away from Rutherglen with all the money we had in the world and Pete immediately volunteered to drive us over to Fernhill.

It was Halloween, nineteen sixty one and my three children came downstairs all painted and shy of the big American stranger who entered the house with a banjo over his shoulder.

His magnificent way with children became immediately apparent as he unstrapped the instrument and his fingers slid over the frets to produce the sweetest music I have ever heard, and he sang for Anna, Matt and Elly the children's songs of Woody Guthrie.

He talked of Woody, a bosom buddy of his who had been born with a serious hereditary ailment called Huntingdon's Chorea, a disease of the grey matter which had been traced back to four English brothers, ancestors of Woody who had settled in America in the eighteenth century, and which disease was currently

Pete Seeger,
with Shonagh, 1965.

destroying one faculty after another in this man who had written songs like 'So Long It's Been Good to Know You', 'The Grand Coolie Dam', 'Deportees' and a thousand others, who had performed with a guitar on which he had painted 'This Machine Kills Fascists' and who among other things had this ability to write simple songs for children, such as Pete was now rendering for mine.

Janette and I attended his concert in the Saint Andrew's Halls which was a magnificent experience with this minstrel, to the great consternation of the hallkeeper, dragging a log on to the stage and chopping it into tiny pieces as an accompaniment to one of his work songs. He described himself as a full time amateur but there was nothing but the professional about this man as, single-handed, he worked the huge audience into a frenzy of good gutsy singalong and created a page of memory to be carried by those attending till their dying day.

His visit to Glasgow was a milestone of the folk revival in Glasgow and it was more than a milestone for me personally.

He left instructions, I was later to understand, with all the authority he could muster and that was considerable in those days, to 'Keep Matt McGinn Singing' and that, in a factionalised phenomenon like the folk revival movement was, proved of considerable importance to me.

This revival had something almost religious about it with as many sects as there were songs to sing, singers to sing them and writers to write them, and the jealousies were hellish.

There were a few who were not interested in politics but very many of us were and most of us had known of one another in the political field. Many of us had been in the Communist Party and some still were and the scars of battle for and against Stalinism were fresh with us.

My own reputation was of a man who had left the Communist Party so often that King Street, where they had their headquarters, were thinking of issuing specially perforated cards to tear up, and who in addition was too fond of a drink, which was unfortunately true. But the blessing of Pete and that of Ewan MacColl who was a very much respected figure among the 'purists' in the field took me into clubs, concerts and even radio programmes throughout Britain and my songs began to be sung by Robin Hall and Jimmie Macgregor, Josh McRae, The Islanders and a very formidable Irish songwriter Dominic Behan, among many many others.

## I.O.U.

Two months after this visit of Pete, a letter arrived from the American Tuning Fork as he had been described inviting me to a tour of the States. 'At the moment I have only been able to arrange one booking for you,' he apologised. 'And that is for a concert in Carnegie Hall, New York, on the Twentieth of October this year.'

I could scarcely believe my eyes. I couldn't play an instrument, and my voice has been adequately described as a fair mixture of lumpy porridge and broken glass and here I was being booked for the world's most celebrated concert hall. Other people had struggled from the bottom for years towards such an objective. Here was I being invited to start at the top. Maybe there was a lesson there. From there on in everything had to be downhill. Until then, however it would be up.

The encouragement of this was breathtaking. I literally churned out songs by the dozen and the score. Some of them were throwaways which would last only for a few months, but others were snaffled up by other singers in and around the folk scene. My aim here was to write longlasters in the hope that some would be absorbed into the tradition.

I was first and foremost a political animal and wrote a great deal on such themes and although I did not always avoid them I did see the danger of being too direct on such matters as social justice.

I could be wrong but I felt that the most effective protest song was of the type produced by writers like Merle Travis in songs like 'The Company Store' whose attack on the system of the Company tying a man's purchasing to its own store, charging exorbitant prices, and thereby having the workers continually in debt to it was of an oblique character which could encourage even nits who didn't even know what they were singing about to make unconscious protestations. Similarly his song, 'Dark as a Dungeon' appealed to me and I did aim perhaps unsuccessfully along these lines. In clubs and concerts I would say, 'This is a song about Hire Purchase to which we are all deeply indebted' and sing my little attemptedly humorous song, 'For an I O I O I O U'.

Attempting to be humorous I could not possibly avoid, all of my own family having wittingly or unwittingly instilled humour into me.

My father's favourite songs had been of the funny Music Hall and usually Cockney type. When he had had a drink he would sing;

> I took my Missus for a walk we met a friend of mine
> He took us into a public house and treated us to wine
> When he called my dear wife outside I thought he must be drunk
> But ten minutes later I looked out and found he'd done a bunk
> But he can't diddle me O no he can't diddle me
> If he takes me for a mug I'll soon let him see
> When he saw the coast was clear he hopped off with my old dear
> But I went back and I drunk his beer he can't diddle me.

My mother too had had an eye and ear for the funny and if Old Nelly came upon a story she believed in exploiting it to the full and extracting the last ounce of comic relief from it by telling it to us at every available opportunity. Like how old Kate Lamb when her mind was wandering with age said to her, 'Oweny came in and told me Mary was dead and Mary came in and told me Oweny was dead and I don't know which one to believe' or about the Jewish man who was struck by the half-drunk Christian. 'What was that for?' said the Jew. 'You're a Jew. You're one of the ones that killed Christ.' 'That was two thousand years ago,' said the Jew. 'Aye, well I only heard about it yesterday,' said the drunk. Then too she had a fund of folk wisdom like her own grandmother's comment on lesbianism that 'Butter to butter's nae kitchen.' Then too I had to compete with my brother Joe who told a Gallowgate fighting man who had him by the throat, 'If it's trouble you're looking for you'll not get it here.'

What was humorous or compassionate in the family history was passed on. For example we learned how my old great grandfather Barney went to the Registrar's Office.

'I've come to register the birth of a child.'

'Is it your child?' said the registrar.

'How would I know that?' says Barney. 'Wouldn't you have to go and ask the mother?'

'You might take off your hat in here.'

'I do to my superior,' says Barney. 'But I never met one of them yet.'

Then too the Gallowgate district where I was born and brought up was full of stories, like Joe the Bull saying to the man, 'Was it you or your brother that had the fatal accident?'

### Blowin' in the wind

It was fourteen years since I had seen my sister Pat and there she was waving to me from the balcony of Idlewide Airport in New York.

I had one more obstacle to surmount before I could cuddle her and I was sure all the way from Prestwick that I would get no further than this.

The United States had not seen the last of McCarthyism and even past membership of the Communist Party was looked upon as a crime, and in addition I was here as the guest of Pete Seeger and Pete had been sentenced to one year's imprisonment by the House Un-American Activities Committee.

True, this savage sentence upon this great instrumentalist who had taught a hundred thousand to play the five-string banjo, this singer who had sent spinning round the world great songs like 'Guantanamera', had now been quashed. But this quashing by the Supreme Court had been on a technicality and he still stood guilty of refusing to name names of people who might have been Communists, of refusing to act as a stool-pigeon for inquisitionists who had destroyed the livelihoods and even lives of thousands of their own countrymen with their blacklists.

Approaching this last hurdle of the Immigration desk, behind which sat a huge red-faced man in a sky blue shirt, a lot less stuffy looking than his Prestwick counterpart, I was saying to myself, 'I hope at least they'll let me see Pat before they put me on the next plane back.'

'That looks like a good bottle of Scotch you got there,' said the blue-shirted man gazing with some apparent longing upon the seven giller I had bought hopefully for my brother-in-law, Neilly Moore, and which I was holding preciously in my right hand as I handed over my passport with my left.

'Would you like some?' says I to the big genial-faced man.

'Yeah,' he said proferring a plastic cup from behind his desk for me to fill which I did, as he put a stamp on my book.

'Have a nice stay,' said he suddenly lightening my heart. Now I would be able to see Pat. My cousin Lizzie Sloan's son, Tommy Robertson was also there and he whisked us off in a Mercedes to Pat's house in Jamaica, New York.

The remainder of that day we spent in Neilly and Pat's house, beng introduced to their neighbours, so it wasn't until the following day that I was able to venture forth to discover God's own country.

'Take that umbrella,' said Pat.

'An umbrella? Me, a Glasgow working man?' 'Take a look out the window.'

I did, to find that although there was a clear blue sky every man, woman and child I could see was carrying an umbrella. So I succumbed and off I went.

In the sun the broad boulevards shone and indeed looked as I had seen them in motion pictures and although I felt that at any time some FBI man would pull me up for my past membership of the Communist Party and deposit me at the airport, I was enjoying looking at the shiny shop fronts of the delicatessens, the fancy goods shops, the drug stores, bars and diners.

Into one of the latter I popped to buy some matches. 'A box of matches please,' I asked of a small Italian-featured man. He looked at me for a second or two as though in disbelief at my request before he reached for the gantry and brought forth a packet of safetys with the name of the diner printed on it.

The Italian looked even more surprised when I gave him a handful of coins from which I expected him to choose whatever I owed him for the matches. Without speaking he waved my money aside.

'How much do I owe you?' I asked and again he refused to accept anything.

After a few more offers and refusals I tumbled that the

Passport, 1962 (renewed 1967).

With sister Pat Moore, Saratoga Springs, 1962.

matches were free for customers buying other goods in the shop and I asked for a cup of coffee.

The following day when Pete Seeger came to collect me to take me to his home upstate in Beacon, I told him about this and he grinned, 'You can tell all the folks back home, Matt, that we in the States got socialised matches.'

We were to go first to the *Sing Out* office downtown New York to meet Irwin Silber the editor of the magazine, Mo Asch the director of Folkways Records, whose office combined with that of *Sing Out*, and a young singer songwriter who had sprung suddenly upon the folk scene, whose name was Zimmerman, alias Bob Dylan.

We discussed the programme for the Carnegie Hall concert and Bob Dylan sang a song which he said he had just written the day before, 'It's a Hard Rain Gonna Fall'.

A slender and fine-featured man, Dylan was obviously bursting with talent but this was a few months before Peter, Paul and Mary would send his song 'Blowin' in the Wind' around the world's wavelengths and send millions of young folk crazy with admiration, taking the folk thing to a new level. At this moment he was still straining at the leash.

St Andrew's Halls, c.1963.

'How would I go in Britain Matt?' he asked later at a social gathering in Greenwich Village.

'A year's time, you'll do it,' says I. 'At the moment your name is filtering through, but it's not there yet.'

Without claiming any great talent as a prophet my words, which were spoken only because I knew something of the scene, did mark a truth. Six months after that party, Dylan did come to Britain and did not cause a ripple. Six months after that he filled the Albert Hall.

At the concert Bob was more than a little nervous, 'Hey Matt, you got any nail clippers?' Needless to say I did not have any. Very few Glasgow men carry them around with them. But if he were nervous the young folk in the audience were even more nervously waiting for him to appear.

The audience was a Pete Seeger crowd, but the younger men and women among them had become aware of this talented young man from the mid-west, whom Pete was encouraging to the top and there was a ripple of excitement as Pete introduced him. I personally had no idea he would be so big, but that audience seemed to sense it.

It was strange, a character like me being on that stage in Carnegie Hall, and it was almost my first paid engagement at a fee of two hundred dollars against Bob Dylan's sixty dollars for the night. A few really talented people work their way from the bottom up to an appearance in that magnificent hall built by Dunfermline's most famous son, with the aid of a few other building workers. But me. Never. I start at the top. From then on it had to be down all the way.


### Bingo Bella

The old Gaiety Theatre at Anderston Cross in Glasgow had gone the road of most cinemas in Britain with the onrush of television and Bingo and when Glasgow's concert hall, namely the Saint Andrew's Halls, near Charing Cross, was destroyed by fire the Corporation decided to use The Gaiety as a temporary alternative. It proved a very temporary alternative as it too was to suffer from a fire. But during its short life it saw a number of combined Jazz and Folk concerts usually organised by Andy Daisley, a man of amazing energy, enterprise, and a cash register brain, who with very little by way of resources had set up his own agency and hardnecked it sufficiently to bring Lou Armstrong, old Satchmo himself, to Glasgow to sing in Ibrox Stadium.

One night he had booked the hall for a concert, the bill including Kenny Ball and his Jazzmen and Archie Fisher who had set Andy into a panic by phoning at the last minute from Edinburgh to say that he had laryngitis.

'What are we gonnie dae?' asked Andy of his aides.

'Get Matt McGinn,' piped up one of them.

'Who's Matt McGinn?' chirped Andy. 'Never heard of him.'

'Folk singer,' he was told.

'Where will we get him?' asked Andy, hope in his blue eyes.

He's up at The Bothy in Bath Street.'

'Right. Get a taxi to the Bothy and ask him to come down here and I'll give him twenty quid for a twenty minute spot,' screamed Andy.

Between my two spots at the Bothy I was taxied down to the concert hall and met Andy in the wings.

'Where's your guitar?' asked Andy desperately.

'I don't use a guitar,' says I.

'Banjo?' says Andy.

'Nothing.'

'Nae accompaniment?' says Andy unbelievingly.

'You mean you go on that stage naked?' said Kenny Ball bewildered.

On Andy went and introduced me and I went on and tore the place apart with 'The Red Yo Yo', 'Three Nights and a Sunday' and a number of other songs plus a few jokes.

The audience went wild and so did Andy.

Two days later in his Tuesday Column in *The Sun* newspaper Forrie Cairns devoted his entire column to a rave write-up on this new songwriting phenomenon of whom he had not heard until now.

Andy, while a good organiser of concerts, did not know that unaccompanied singers even the one who had torn that concert hall apart could not just be thrown on to any old stage and do the same. He started booking me into places like Bingo Halls and Beat Clubs.

In Strathclyde Bingo Hall in Bridgeton I was thrown to the lions, a crowd of people who wouldn't have listened to the Great

With Matt junior and Tom Paxton, 1962.

Caruso singing with the Hollywood Bowl behind them and who certainly were not interested in listening to a little nyaff like me sing in a gravelly voice songs of a folksy nature.

'Get aff the stage.' 'Who the hell told you you could sing?' I suffered and endured until the manager mercifully beckoned me off.

It was not my scene, nor was The Clelland Bar in the Gorbals which specialised in Beat groups. I sat terrified as I watched three beat groups do their stuff before I was due on stage. The third group was just leaving the stage when Andy nudged me. 'On you go now.'

'Are you no introducing me?' said I in horror.

'No. On you go yersel,' said Andy and on I went to face an audience who thought I had just wandered in off the street. With great courage and fortitude I had croaked my way throught the 'Yo Yo', and 'MacPerson's Rant' and was on the first verse of 'Rosin the Bow' when I saw it arise right at the back of the long hall and move menacingly, a brute of a man with a sunburst of Ireland face and shoulders which could have heaved down the Tron steeple.

'Who the fucking hell told you you could sing?' he bellowed.

'I'm just finishing,' says I and shuffled back to Andy's side, there to sit sheepishly till an opportune moment arose to creep out of the Lounge to the safety of the Gorbals street.

We learned, and Andy did organise some successful folk concerts with me but I have never forgotten those terrors.

## Manura Manya

The Marland Bar had sung, for over a century, songs of Scottish exile, 'In fancy I can see her noo', and of Irish invasion, 'Here I am from Paddy's land', but its sweetest songs it reserved for its dying days. In the redeveloping Glasgow of the fifties and sixties the pubs of George Street lost most of their regular customers and the Marland was no exception to the general rule, but it found a new clientele in the crowds of Folksong revivalists who hit Glasgow in the sixties and who, under the leadership of young Andrew Moyes had established a folk centre nearby in Montrose Street. The majority of members being of the thirsty variety and there being 'Nae Booze' allowed in the centre they needed a local pub.

The Dunrobin would have been suitable but the management did not wish to have these Beatniks with their strange songs. Besides they still had a clientele in the *Scottish Daily Express* staff. In the Marland, Chris the proprietor was more amenable to the folksies and to our songs and our money and in we came to sing the 'Swan Song' of the Marland.

Leading off the singing one Saturday evening was my friend Hamish Imlach a genial bright-eyed and heavily built man and Peter Ross, a young law office worker.

> Wi me toorininya wi me toorininya wi me toorininyoorin in
> yoorin in ya .

They sang 'The Kerry Recruit' in a haunting manner which lingered even after the company had moved on to, 'We're gonna roll the Union on'. With a drink in me I murmured something about none of them being in a Union and within a few minutes Hamish was roused from his normal joviality to a fiery rage in which he was threatening to carry me outside the pub and do all sorts of things to my snozzle and I suddenly sobered to the fact that this man was no flab but a physical power-house who could have massacred me with a couple of punches.

I was pleased when he was asked by one of the staff to leave the premises and I took over the leading of the singing from that moment, which was about half past eight.

At ten past ten as I was being emptied from the pub with the rest of the spillage, Hamish came rushing at me from the other side of the street where he had been waiting all this time for me to have 'a discussion'. Fortunately for me there were enough there to separate us and when forty of them had gotten round Hamish the other one took me by the elbow and guided me towards my bus.

At home in Fernhill I said, 'To hell wi' them and their toorininya . . . .' But I decided to do a real job on the 'to hell wi'' and wrote:

> Wi' manura manya, wi' manura manya
> Wi' manura manura manura manya

The chorus should be sung sweetly and with feeling. Although here a word of warning. I was singing this song at Ledlanet House in Kinross during one of their cultural seasons and I asked the audience to harmonise not knowing that half of them were from an opera company which was there to rehearse for their own *Barber of Seville* the following evening. And boy did they harmonise:

68

> I have heard men complain of the jobs that they're daein'
> When they're howking the coal and they're digging the drain
> But whatever they are there is none can compar'
> Wi' the man that's oot shovellin' manura manya

You will have gathered that this is a protest song about the transport revolution which has transformed Glasgow into a one horse town.

Pete Seeger snatched up that song and sang it at the Newport Festival on the conclusion of his world tour, and according to Luke Kelly of the Dubliners who was there it set the place ablaze. Later Pete recorded it at Carnegie Hall and I still get an occasional tenner from Japan for this. His recording of it is played from time to time in Tokyo where I often picture the locals going around singing about horse manure.

Money from abroad, there's a strange thing. I once received money from an American publisher who said he had gotten it from a German distributor who had ascribed to me the writing of 'MacPherson's Rant'. This being back in my more honest days I returned the money with a note:

> I am sorry I cannot claim the copyright on MacPherson's
> Rant which was written in 1701 but if you are interested in
> 'The King Sits In Dunfermline Toon Drinking The Blood Red
> Wine' which I wrote when I was a boy in Twelve Ninety Six
> ascription can be arranged.

As a Scottish Irish mongrel and proud of it I had got to thinking about the Jewish people and about how if I were Jewish I would be equally proud of a people, who, in spite of having their fair share of rogues have also produced so many of the basic truth seekers and influence makers of the ages, Moses, Christ, Marx, Freud, Einstein. I wrote:

> My faither was born a Hebrew My faither was born a Jew
> My faither was born a Hebrew and I'm a Hebrew too.

I sang this song in Carnegie Hall, to a mainly Jewish audience. It's difficult to get any other kind of audience in New York.

They were giving the chorus pelters and I was pleased to think they were able to understand my meaning till afterwards a Young All American Jewish girl came back stage and interrupted a conversation I was having with Bob Dylan, and she says, 'That was a wonderful song, "My faither was born a Hebrew". But tell me, what does faither mean?'

However I'm glad to say that another Jew in the audience, the famous film actor Theodore K. Bikel, got the full meaning of the song, liked it and sung it all over the States, and I understand explains to his audience the meaning of faither every time he does so.

### Phil was rid wi rage

I remember singing in a folk song club in the Lake District which was run by a nymphomaniac, whose company I enjoyed. She was a great conversationalist.

Anyway, I was making some jokes about the English and the mainly English audience were taking it in good spirits.

'By the way' says I, 'my making fun of the English is not to be taken as a sign of any great courage on my part. It's just that I find your people can laugh at themselves much quicker than my own folk can.' There was a bit too much applause at this so I said, 'Mind you, you've more to laugh at.'

This was at the time in the sixties when the folk song business was almost a religion to some folk and there were some indeed in these clubs who disliked entirely the idea of joke telling and laughter in the hallowed halls of traditional come allye's and who wished only to hear miserable sounding songs about the conditions of fourteenth century seamen and such. There were also those, usually the same type of people, who argued that a folk song was not a folk song unless it was a couple of hundred years old.

Since I was in the habit of cracking jokes and since I found difficulty in writing two hundred year old songs I fell foul of many of the organisers of some clubs. However, I found that I was able to break out beyond the folk scene proper and more into a kind of cabaret act with the concentration more and more on humour and less on the political protest type of song, which privately I still often prefer but which always seemed to get me into trouble. Take the song I wrote about the Duke of Edinburgh and sang to him in Cardiff.

At the Commonwealth Arts Festival in that town in September nineteen sixty five I was taking part in a play which had been

Vol 4 No 4        Price 1⁄6

# CHAPBOOK

Scotland's Folk-Life Magazine

MATT McGINN
SPECIAL ISSUE

Special issue of *Chapbook,* 1967.

written by C.P. Taylor and then cocked up so much by the little American producer that at the end of its opening performance Taylor stood up in the auditorium and denounced what he had just seen as bearing no resemblance to what he had written.

To that opening performance The Duke of Edinburgh had accepted an invitation. But when the Arts Director saw the play in rehearsal this proposed visit of the Duke to the theatre was cancelled.

It would in fact have been ridiculous for the Duke to have been asked to sit through scenes introduced by the producer where they were showing the Queen on tour in India while I was to sit at the side of the stage singing Manura Manya.

In common with all those taking part in the festival the cast of our play was invited to a reception given by the Mayoress of Cardiff at which we were to be introduced to the Royal personage.

There was a great deal of plonk in the hall and I consumed a good deal of the stuff. I must in fact have been slightly tipsy when the principal guest was shepherded to the corner where I was standing with a tall young English girl from the cast of our play which was called 'Of Hope and Glory'.

'Keep that man away,' the mayoress said to the chief constable who was there without his uniform but with a chest full of medals and other decorations. With an enormous elbow the policeman edged me aside.

But he was too late. The Duke's hand was out and vacant and I clasped it, placing my left hand on his shoulder so that the big man was trapped.

'They're trying to stop me from shaking hands with you, and you know I wrote a song about you that one day might make you famous,' says I as he looked a little uncomfortably from down on me to up at my companion.

'It's a good song,' says she, seemingly easing the Duke's mind. Then I sang:

> Oor Phil's a big time hunter
> He doesnae know nae fear
> He went wi' Liz to India
> And he shot a tiger there
> The first six shots misfired
> Phil was red wi' rage
> So they took him to the Bombay zoo
> And he shot one in a cage

With Shonagh, 1966.

'What's the point?' says he.

'Good wee song,' says I. 'Isn't it?'

'Does he sing that song in that play?' the Duke asked the girl.

'No,' says I. 'But if you come and see it tomorrow I'll give a special performance of it.'

'I'm afraid I've got to be somewhere else tomorrow with other engagements.'

'Cancel them,' says I, 'and come round and see the play.'

'I'd better go,' said the Duke, 'before I do something that will make you famous.'

I continued with my celebration of the fact that our daughter Shonagh had been born that day, the Seventeenth of September.

From record sleeve of *Screwtops are Falling on my Head,* 1975.

### The Two-Heided Man

'The Two-Heided Man' album, my first really big seller, I recorded at the Police Club in Edinburgh, but in the most painful circumstances.

The tickets for the session, which was to be 'Live', had immediately been snatched up, as I had always gone down well in the club – which was why I had chosen to make the LP there.

Mervyn Solomon, the director of the Belfast-based Emerald Gem record company had approached Pete Kerr with a view to getting me to record a humorous album.

Pete told me that Mervyn had already approached several

Scottish comedians about making such an album, including Lex McLean. Lex had refused on the grounds that it ran away with too much material, which I think a pity, now that my friend Lex has departed. Among the Greats of Scottish comedy, Lex, had he accepted the offer, could have left us an album which would have been treasured for a long time to come. For myself, I was free of contracts at the time and accepted the challenge willingly.

But then the snags arose, the first and biggest of all arising from an announcement, a few days before the session was due, that on that very night television would be giving live coverage to the two European championship games in which Rangers and Celtic were involved. With this, the tickets for the recording session began flooding back to the club steward's office till we were left with a three quarters empty hall and an immediately depressing atmosphere.

I had a fine folk group from Fife, The Waverleys, with me and in the circumstances they did a great job. But we had not had enough time for rehearsals and in addition I had not yet developed the sense that it is inadvisable to drink and work, and I had had a few pints during the session.

I had enough sense to see from my end that we were not getting a recording out of it and began dragging material from the soles of my shoes, and found that the naughtier the material the better things were going, so I went from naughty to downright uncouth.

I did not go so far as the young idiot of a folk singer who I had seen a few years back physically lifted from a stage and thrown out of the hotel, for not understanding that what you can sing out there among the sheep is not necessarily what you can render in a company.

He was prancing about the stage with a guitar and singing:

> I've been a sheep drover for many a year
> Wi my wee Collie dug I aye take up the rear
> I'm driving them to and I'm driving them fro
> Where I'm driving these sheep I just don't fucking know
> And it's sheep's heid and liver
> Sheep's heid liver and lamb
> Won't someone please tell me
> Where the fucking hell I am

He was on the centre of the stage waving his guitar wildly, trying unsuccessfully to involve the audience in his obscene songs the words of which it seemed he had written that morning while taking care of his ablutions.

'Away and hoo yerself,' he shouted at the crowd, acknowledging their jeers. 'I've got to making a living int ah. You're no denying a man a livelihood are you?'

With this there were shouts of, 'Die Die Die,' as half a dozen men jumped on to the stage to remove the poor demented man.

Demented as I obviously have been all these years to put myself in my present predicament, I did not on this occasion go so far as this young man but I did do my poem the Big Effen Bee and went from that to the Dogs' Party which is an explanation in song of why dogs sniff one another.

The audience had been cold to begin with and had they not numbered among them a few men, and even more particularly women with really dirty laughs they might have remained that way. But they warmed, or otherwise we might have had a complete and utter disaster.

As it was, at the end of the night Bryce Laing who was assisting Pete Kerr on the technical side was very doubtful if we had a record. Pete, a little more confident on the score, was still not without doubts, and I was depressed on my way home to Rutherglen.

However, when a few days later we got together in Waverley Studio Pete did such an excellent job on the tape cutting and editing that we had a cracker of a record which was put out through Decca.

The sales at first were poor and in fact Emerald Gem who had an option of a further year with me dropped it and were in no way interested in having me make another record with them.

Then, strangely and solely by word of mouth it took off by leaps and bounds so that now, years later, it is a standard order for most record shops and is to be found in the homes of most expatriate Scots in Canada, Australia, and the States.

At first it had seemed that only policemen were buying it, their interest being aroused by the fact that it had been recorded in a police club and by the fact that it contained in one of the poems there recorded a line about a 'Big Effen Polis'.

That poem would get me into trouble on many an occasion, as

With accompanist Billy Davidson, early 1970s.

for example when one night in the Westwood in East Kilbride two policemen entered just as I was reciting it and the head bummer of the two threatened to have me arrested on a charge of inciting a riot. But most policemen seemed to be tickled by the totally harmless piece of nonsense.

Then too the record had begun to cause laughter among freemasons and Knights of Saint Columba through another piece of rubbish I had put on the record, namely 'Saint Columba and

In characteristic pose, 1972.

The Masons', which song Billy Connolly, Tom Harvey and myself had penned in my house in Rutherglen:

> Tubal Cain was a mason a square dealing man
> He was aye on the level wi' the shake o' the hand
> Wi' his feet at right angles he was sure he'd go far
> Nonchalantly giving signals as he stood at the bar
> Tell me Who is yer Granny he signalled to me
> As he rolled up his troosers to expose his left knee
> He was good at the folk songs he preferred them to Jazz
> And his favourite folk singer they called Joan Boaz
> But it cost him a fortune for these secret delights
> So he told me last Tuesday he's joining the Knights of Saint Columba

So the record had broken through.

Two years later I approached Mervyn Solomon and found he was only too interested in a follow-up, 'The Two-Heided Man Strikes Again', which has proven equally successful.


### The Big Effen Bee

On the third of October nineteen seventy five the newspapers were full of it.

'Roll up, roll up for the Great Sheriff Court Show, starring at great expense (to himself) Matt McGinn, who described himself as Novelist, Songwriter, Comedian,' ran *The Scotsman*.

'How the Sheriff learned about the Bees,' headlined *The Daily Record*. *The Daily Express*, which also did a very humorous piece on the Sheriff Court Show, printed a small poster with my face on it, declaring 'Wanted, for Flybillposting.'

The Scottish press and a large part of the English plus Radios Clyde and Forth, Scottish Television and even the pussyfooting BBC Television rose to the occasion and treated the Great Sheriff Court Show as the comic opera farce by which term I described it in Court.

Charged with having displayed posters on sites throughout the city without the permission of the owners of the said sites, I was found not guilty of putting up the posters but guilty of refusing to get them down, and fined thirty pounds.

The posters, fifty one of which were mentioned, had appeared on walls and hoardings one night almost a year before, advertising two Long Playing records and reading in part 'Matt McGinn's

Fantastic New LP, "The Two-Heided Man Strikes Again". (The Big 'Shike) the follow-up to "The Two-Heided Man", (The Big Effen Bee), on sale at Woolworths, Boots and other record shops.'

Now Glasgow was full of such illegal poster advertisements informing the world that certain wares were available to people, such as Datsun cars at so and so garage, demonstrations to be held for and against abortion and telling of meetings where one could hear Harry McShane talking on unemployment or Yoko Hami on Karate or Paul Foot on how easy it would be to have a revolution next Tuesday at half-past-two provided it weren't raining. There were literally thousands of them with as many names on them. But these ones with my name on them seemed to be special for some people, and on the basis of them some persons in Glasgow City Chambers decided to pounce.

For those Chambers I have never had a great deal of respect. That well-known character The Clincher, had more respect for them than I. He was a hairdresser from the Maryhill district of the city whom certain officials connected with those chambers had at one time tried to have declared insane.

The doctor at Hawkhead asylum to which he had been referred by one of the magistrates for examination stated that The Clincher was as sane as he himself was, to which The Clincher had retorted, 'Could you give me a written statement to that effect?'

From then on The Clincher, whom I remember seeing standing in the Trongate roaring and bawling about 'The municipal Chamber and those who sit in it', developed the habit of holding up this doctor's letter and shouting, 'I am the only sane man in Glasgow with a certificate to prove it.'

In attacking the people connected with George Square he was expressing the disrespect which most Glaswegians have for these bureaucrats, if we are to judge by the fact that a thirty per cent poll at a municipal election is considered massive, but such attacks merited in their eyes special treatment for The Clincher, and like The Clincher I was to be singled out for extraordinary action.

The other posters might be objectionable but the ones with McGinn's name on them were outright obnoxious.

The telephone rang in my Rutherglen home.

'I would like to speak to Mister Matt McGinn,' a voice said.

'Speaking,' says I.

'This is a Mister Cumming of Glasgow Corporation Planning

Department,' said the voice, shocking me with the news that Glasgow had a Planning Department. Until then I had thought that those bloody great concrete jungles and deserts like The Calton and Dalmarnock and Partick had arisen by accident.

'What's your first name'? says I.

'I don't think we'll be on first name terms,' says the voice.

'What's your first name?' I insisted, finally eliciting the information that it was Andrew.

'Hello Andy', says I, still thinking I was being phoned regarding an engagement.

'A number of posters have appeared throughout the city,' said the voice, 'advertising records of yours and I am phoning to warn you that if they are not taken down in the next seven days you will be prosecuted under the terms of the Town and Country Planning Act.'

'I never put them up,' says I.

'Your name is on them,' said the voice.

'I've seen them,' says I, 'but I never put them up.'

'Who did put them up?' asked the voice.

'I don't know,' says I, 'but I've an idea who might have done and I'll pass on your message to them.'

Some days later an official letter arrived from Cumming or Cummings indicating that he had done some considerable homework on these posters and that he or someone else had been spending a great deal of ratepayers' money in touring the city looking for posters with my name on them, singling them out from a million others and threatening prosecution if I did not have them removed.

From previous experience in political campaigns I knew that pasting posters illegally is a tricky business and the business of taking them down proved every bit as tricky or even more so. Apart from the businesss of not being caught by the police there is the technical thing which makes taking a poster from a wall or boarding a great deal more difficult than pasting it up.

However, I did not wish to have a clash with the law and after midnight that night, equipped with a paint scraper, I headed for Waterloo Street where I had seen a number of these posters on the front of a disused shop. In my own opinion the posters actually enchanced the appearance of the broken-down building but they were nonetheless illegal. There was even an inscription on the shop front, saying 'Bill Stickers will be prosecuted,' under which someone had written, 'Bill Stickers is Not Guilty'.

So was I, not guilty, but desirous of steering clear of the courts I set to with the scraper. I had not managed to remove four square inches of the first poster when a policeman's torch shone on me.

'What have we here?' said the Bobby.

'I'm trying to take down this poster,' says I.

'Have you the permission of the owner of these premises?' says the Bobby.

'No, I'm afraid not,' says I. 'But I've been instructed to get them down by Glasgow Corporation.'

'Get on your way,' says he, 'or I'll arrest you for defacing that wall or even worse.'

So with the scraper in my pocket and my good intention in the soles of my shoes I headed for a taxi at the Central Station and then home to Rutherglen.

A few days later an urgent telegram arrived from Mervyn Solomon of Emerald Gem Records in Belfast which caused me to panic and to rethink the whole business:

'Telephone Glasgow's Chief Constable regarding posters on walls in Glasgow.'

This was getting serious. Here were Glasgow police at the highest level getting in touch with Belfast police, presumably at a similarly high level, in connection with these posters.

I would have to earnestly consider this matter which was upsetting the authorities so much that Glasgow's Chief Constable who had hold-ups, murders, rapes, Christmas shoplifting, drugtaking and trafficking, breaches of the peace, burglaries and assaults to occupy his mind getting in touch with Belfast where there had been five killings, two kneecappings and fourteen buildings blown up the previous day. I conjured up a picture of a Calling all Cars in Northern Ireland. 'Be on the lookout for any evidence connected with some serious flybillposting which has been going on in the city of Glasgow, advertising two very dangerous long playing records by one Matt McGinn, a troublesome resident of the No Mean City'.

My heavens, this was getting out of hand. I looked out of the window for the posse and was relieved to see none.

'We'd better have a look at these posters,' I said to Janette and we got into her car to drive through the city on a tour similar to that in which the Glasgow Corporation officials must have been engaged.

What we found was truly alarming. At the corner of Cathcart and Aitkenhead Roads there were two of these black and yellow posters in among another forty three advertising concerts and meetings on the walls of a bank which had only just been closed for five and a half years. These posters with my name on them must have been a dreadful eyesore to the squatters who were living without electricity in the tenement flats above and to the rat which we saw crawling out of the close nearby. The seven we saw on the shop front in Waterloo Street would definitely be causing physical pain to the building workers who were digging foundations for another building opposite.

But the really torturous one of these posters for the Glasgow Corporation officials must surely have been the one we found stuck on its side to a piece of broken masonry at the corner of North Frederick and George Streets. So much suffering had this apparently caused that they had actually gone to the trouble of demolishing the building the day before. A terrible feeling of shame and guilt fell upon me as I thought of all the anguish which these posters were causing these officials, who surely had enough on their plate what with attending conferences in Stockholm and Chicago, authorising artists' grants to study graffiti in New York and awarding licences to Reo Stakis;

Reo Stakis belongs to Glasgow
Dear old Glasgow Town
Nae wonder he grins with his Old Worlde Inns
He's worth ten million pounds
He was only a common old working chap
Till he found the golden geese
But now with the George Square stretched out before him
He'll no be goin' back to Greece.

My one consolation was that I had not paid for, had not ordered and had not pasted or displayed the posters. So I let the matter slip from my mind with the additional balmy thought that there was so much sense and justice in Scotland that any attempted prosecution would be thrown out of court on the principle that a person is innocent until proven guilty.

How wrong I was!

## A Square Dealin Man

Two policemen arrived at the door with a summons compelling me to appear at the Sheriff Court in Ingram Street. The court building itself is a miserable place with which I have painful associations of mind and the mere sight of the summons brought to memory the angry little procurator fiscals who must surely be the most painful people in the world to live with, being in constant accusation of their fellow men, and of judges whose minds are filled with their own sense of power and influence and of defence lawyers in constant cahoots with judges and procurators, all of them running around like bats in their black satin capes, the only thing to distinguish them from the little knots of unfortunates they are there to pass judgement upon. It was from this miserable building that I had been taken as a twelve year old to Saint Mary's. More recently I had spent six or seven hours in its cells, which are not fit to keep wild dogs in, never mind human beings.

On that occasion I had gotten myself into trouble with the Insurance people over the matter of self-employed stamps. Until a couple of years before I had always been employed by others, as a message boy, a blacksmith's assistant, hod carrier and navvy, whisky bond porter, bird cage factory worker, machine operator and school-teacher and in all these occupations your stamps are secured and taken care of by the employer. But then I had gone full-time acting, singing and writing and now came into the category of 'Self-Employed'. The rule which should be followed here is to buy a self-employed or non-employed stamp each week, as the case may be, and this I neglected in the knowledge that in this category as in others the stamp card is sent to the authority concerned once a year.

At the end of the year I found myself once again skint and a little Social Security man, a five foot two 'Detective' came to see me. I explained the circumstances and at first the little man was fine about it and agreed that I should pay off the arrears at so much a week. Then this little tuppence ha'penny clerk started to wag a finger in my face. 'Now Matthew, on this occasion we will allow you to pay up this way but if this happens again you will be taken to court.' His little uncalloused finger was almost up my nose and angered me into an outburst:

'You go ahead and take me to court and don't point your

finger at a holy picture.' It was enough to start a battle between myself and all the clerks and clerkesses in Dalmarnock Road Social Security Offices and the moment I fell behind with the agreed weekly sum they charged like Bruce at Bannockburn.

I did not know then that a debt to the Pensions Board is not in the category of a civil debt but comes under the classification of a Crime, and in fact 'Fraud' is the involved offence. So there was a shocker for me one night when I came home after singing at a folk concert in the Burnside Hotel.

'The Rutherglen police phoned up,' said Janette. 'They said they have a warrant for your arrest but they didn't want to embarrass you by taking you in. So you've to go down there at half-past-eight in the morning and see them.' The shock did not really sink in then. I was still in the foolish habit of having a drink in the premises I had been singing in and we had had a few. The effect of the alcohol was to shield me momentarily from the shattering news.

But shattered I was when I arrived at Rutherglen Police Office to find I was charged with Fraud. I was locked up then for half an hour with a clown who seemed quite proud that he as an ex-postman was there on a charge of stealing postal orders from letters. In addition to his unpleasant company there was the sight of a torn and unrinated-on mattress in the cell. I wondered if the Rutherglen councillors ever visited the Police Office to examine these cells, but knowing some of them and seeing this one I concluded, No. But if this were unpleasant I had still worse to come. After half an hour a police van arrived and a very officious red-headed policeman tightened his fist on the cuff of my jacket and lumbered me in to take me out in the same manner at the Sheriff Court. A desk sergeant looked up at me in some surprise when he read the charge sheet.

'Matt,' he said seemingly stunned. 'What the hell are you doing in here?' He was a man in his forties with a tough but sympathetic face.

'It's to do with self-employed Insurance Stamps,' says I.

'Christ, I've got all your records,' he said taking a bunch of keys from behind the desk and leading me along. 'I'll have to lock you up,' he said reluctantly. The cell into which he led me was a box, a windowless crate and no more than eight feet by four by eight feet high. In this there were already four men, cramped and unhappy. One was on a charge of Serious Assault, another on a charge of Burglary and the other two undeclared to me. I was kept in there for about four hours while my name was obviously being bandied about among the policemen. Obviously, because one came along and opened the cell door. 'McGinn,' he called in a stern voice and then took me into the corridor and said quietly, 'Here take these,' and handed me a packet of cigarettes and matches. A little while later another opened the cell, called me out and did similarly with a packet of chewing gum.

Shortly after this I was taken out to be asked if I wanted a lawyer to defend me and I refused. My intention was to obey the golden rule and plead Not Guilty. I did not realise the seriousness of my position or I would have readily agreed to having a lawyer defend me.

Fortunately my wife Janette had a full appreciation of the situation and by the time I was brought before the court she had contacted the Glasgow lawyer Ross Harper and had fully explained the position to him, that I had been paying the arrears as fast as I could. She furnished him with receipts plus the remaining thirty pounds which was owed. Sadly, I had been unaware of Janette's efforts and had, in the agony of that cramped cell, decided I would plead guilty because I had become afraid that if I had ventured a plea of 'Not Guilty' I might be remanded 'in custody', which I thought would have killed me. With a plea of guilty I thought I would be fined and that would be that.

When I entered the dock, Ross Harper turned to me and said, 'Are you pleading Not Guilty' and looked a little shocked when I said, 'Guilty'. He could not argue with me in court or I suspect his advice would have been to plead otherwise. As it was he did a very good job in the circumstances and drew the Court's attention to the fact that had it been any other kind of debt in this country this would be a civil matter and not a criminal one. He also was able to point out on the basis of the receipts which Janette had given him that all that I owed them was thirty pounds instead of the seventy with which I had been charged. The judge wanted time to discuss the matter with the lawyers and I was meantime returned to the cells.

This time the desk sergeant was able to offer the ultimate in privileges, one much greater than even the cigarettes and chewing gum, which were in themselves precious, 'Would you like a single cell, Matt?' he asked 'I'd like that,' I said and spent the rest of the time waiting for my return to the court, where I would be fined twenty pounds, walking up and down the private little box making up a song about John Lennon and Yoko which couldn't have been a very good one, for while I was able to recite it to newspapermen who interviewed me after the trial I have now forgotten the words and the music. But I do remember it was a useful way of passing the time. There was considerable publicity around that Insurance Stamp trial, publicity which I did not like.

There are fools in the entertainment business who believe that no publicity is bad publicity and all publicity is good. I do not share their belief. But this poster business was different and I was determined I would get the maximum coverage on it and I had lots of ammunition to fire.

At the pleading diet I sat at the back of the small courtroom and waited and as I waited, watched and listened to the cases being tried before mine. There were fifteen of these other cases and sentences were imposed for Drunken Driving, not paying television licences and other similar offences, to which all of the accused pled guilty. I noticed that all of the accused called the Sheriff 'Sir' or 'Your Honour' while the procurator kept Milording and that all the accused were asked, 'Do you understand the charge?' I had been a little upset at having being called to the court for 10 o'clock and then having to sit through all these other cases but now, when I was called, I was glad of this.

'Matthew McGinn,' called the clerk of the court and I moved to the top of the long table and looked up at the bewigged Sheriff, thinking it ridiculous, that in this day and age these wigs should be worn and wondering, 'Why oh why?' Surely they can't all be baldy.

'Are you Matthew McGinn?' came the question.

'I am Matthew Moffat Callender McGinn,' said I. 'I answer to Matthew McGinn even when the Matthew is misspelt with a single "t".'

There was something of a flurry in the court and papers started to be moved here and there as for almost a full minute there was otherwise silence. Only the sheriff kept his cool and glanced at the charge sheet and then at me.

'Do you answer to Matthew McGinn when it is spelt with a double "t"?'

'I do, Milord,' said I.

Raising this matter in this way was my way of protesting at the gross misspelling which had occurred in the summons. Most people in the country have read the bible, and should be well aware of how to spell correctly the name of one of its most famous authors.

'You have the middle names Moffat Callender?' said the Sheriff.

'I do, Milord,' said I, saying nothing of the fact that I had just that moment adopted them.

'Do you understand the charge?' the sheriff asked.

'Milord,' I replied, 'I do not understand the charge.'

There was another flurry in the court.

'You do not understand the charge?' said the sheriff.

'I do not understand the charge, Milord,' said I.

'You can read?' said the sheriff.

'I can read, Milord,' I answered.

'But you do not understand the charge?' the sheriff said, seemingly unbelievingly.

'I do not understand the charge, Milord,' said I. 'But I do believe I am entitled to have the charge read out in full before the court.'

'Have a look at the summons,' says he and I obeyed as he went through the first two pages quickly with me and then turned to page three which was the one referring to the Big Effen Bee and the Big Shike which was the one I wanted the court to hear about. But whether the Sheriff knew this or not he would not oblige, but instead asked once more if I understood the charge. I hesitated a moment because I did so much want to hear the court discussing the Big Effen Bees and Big Shikes. But I was wary of the dangers of being held in contempt.

'Yes, Milord, I do,' says I.

'Do you plead guilty or not guilty?' asked the Sheriff.

'I am utterly and completely innocent,' says I. I was going to add, 'And besides that I didn't do it,' but then there would have been little question as to my being held in contempt so I clipped my lips.

'Trial is set for the second of October here at 10.00 a.m. No further notice will be given of this,' said the clerk of court.

'You would be well advised to see a lawyer and enquire as to legal aid,' said the judge.

'Milord,' says I, 'I do not need a lawyer. I do not require legal aid. But perhaps you could advise me as to how I would go about citing as material witnesses, Teddy Taylor M.P., Winifred Ewing M.P., every councillor in Glasgow and several entertainers throughout Scotland.'

'I cannot advise you on these matters. I would advise you to see a lawyer,' said he.

'Thank you, Milord,' said I and I left the court with my son Matt and headed for Albion Street where I gave the story to *The Scottish Daily News* who printed it under the heading 'I'll call M.P.s says Matt'.

It would be three months before the trial and during this time I considered how I should tackle the case and whether in fact I should cite these people I had mentioned, which I considered myself fully justified in doing. After all, there cannot be a Member of Parliament in the country who has not had his name plastered on some wall or other and illegally to boot and there are few councillors who would ever have been elected and fewer entertainers who would have been successful without some flybill-posting. No one is stupid enough to think that they themselves had done the posting or pasting. But here was I to be considered in a different category. In further consideration and after Billy Connolly had agreed to come forward as a witness I decided that I would make Billy the only witness I would call. Billy I felt owed me a favour, my having been responsible for all his first big breaks, taking him as a very talented lad to accompany me in the Close Theatre for three weeks of the play 'Clydeside', for five weeks to accompany me in the Metropole Theatre, on to my programme for BBC television 'Matt McGinn Minstrel', to accompany me on my second full L.P. 'Matt McGinn Again', and having introduced him and Tom Harvey as The Humblebums to Nat Joseph and Transatlantic records. On all of the occasions in which they accompanied me I had always insisted on them being given the opportunity to do their own spot in which they could display their talent.

But it was not just as a favour Billy agreed to act as a witness. He is as most people in Britain are now well aware a man with an eye for publicity himself and it would be quite a stunt as we both agreed in conversation in The Third Eye Centre in Sauchiehall Street.

He would be on tour in England when the trial came up and would catch a helicopter to Glasgow, come to the Sheriff Court to be called to the stand, to be asked by me a single question, 'Have you ever seen your name posted obviously illegally on walls or boardings when and where you had no responsibility for displaying them?' He would answer truthfully, 'Yes' and then hop back to England to finish his tour of England leaving behind a blaze of publicity which would hit all the media in one day. Billy moved house just shortly after we'd discussed this and I did not have his new telephone number so the matter had to be dropped.


### The minister's daughter she was there

So now I had to settle for no witnesses being called by myself. My son, Matt, took care of the press side of things. The press had, in general, been fair to me down the years. I recalled the *Scottish Daily Express*, then being printed in Scotland, and their treatment of an unfortunate incident which could have caused me a great deal more embarrassment than it did simply by their clever use of a headline.

I had been singing for years in folk clubs, and they are a very useful training ground, but they can also have a spoiling effect. Crude and often naughty songs were enjoyed by all who attended these clubs as long as they were in some way clever and a word like 'arsehole' was not likely to be new or offensive to such as the club audiences. So there was one song which I had introduced into the clubs which soon became much requested, namely 'The Dogs' Party' which is in the naughty-but-clever category. It was an old soldiers' song which I had heard as a boy but of which I had forgotten the words until my memory of them was refreshed by Tom Paxton who had heard the same song in the States. The song was okay for the clubs where it always went down a bomb. It was, however, unsuitable for concerts where there was a mixed company, particularly in a respectable place like Aberdeen.

In a big hall in that town Archie Fisher and I were giving a performance and we had taken the place by storm, and I had them rolling in the aisles with songs such as one I had written on their then recent typhoid epidemic in the town:

> I was put in a can, a tiny wee can oot in the Argentine,
> The government man he looked at the can and said, 'Send it to Aberdeen.'
> They're washing their hands in old Aberdeen
> They're scrubbing away all the grit
> It's the queerest thing you've ever seen
> They've put paper in every toilet
> The government told us they werenae to blame
> And they said that their ain hands were clean
> But would you like to dare sell a Fray Bentos share
> In the town of Aberdeen
> I'm only a germ, a tiny wee germ
> The nastiest you've ever seen
> But if you say, 'Hello germ,' I'll no dae nae hairm
> I'll pass on and say, 'Hi Gene!'

At the end of the evening the capacity audience were encoring me and someone shouted for 'The Dogs' Party'.

'Give us "The Dogs' Party",' the shout came from more people in the auditorium.

'Naw, I'm sorry,' says I, 'it's a mixed audience.'

'Give us "The Dogs' Party",' the entire audience seemed to be shouting, those who knew the song wanting it, and those who didn't apparently wondering what I was refusing to sing.

I had no intention of acceding to the request, or more properly the demand that I sing the song until my friend Arthur Argo, who had organised the concert came from backstage into the auditorium and shouted, 'Don't sing it Matt, you'll get me hung!' With this something clicked and I said, 'Aw bugger you Arthur,' and sang:

> The dogs they had a party
> They came from near and far
> And some dogs came by aeroplane
> And some by motor car
> They went into the lobby
> And signed the visitors' book
> And each one hung his arsehole
> Upon a separate hook
> One dog was not invited
> And this aroused his ire
> He rushed into the meeting place
> And loudly shouted, 'Fire!'
> Now the dogs were so excited

They had no time to look
And each one took an arsehole
From off the nearest hook
It is a sad sad story
For it is very sore
To wear another's arsehole
You've never worn before
And that is why when dogs meet
By land or sea or foam
Each sniffs the other's arsehole
In hope it is its own

The entire audience seemed to go into hysterical laughter, but at least one person in the auditorium was offended and seriously so. He was a minister who was there with his sixteen year old daughter and he raised the matter publicly the following day.

Arriving in Glasgow two days after the concert I phoned Janette, to be told, 'The press is all about you, you'd better contact the *Express* who haven't been off the phone for the past twenty four hours.' I did phone the *Express* and the following day they had a front page story, with their sports editor suggesting the headline, 'Oh the minister's daughter she was there' which was of course a quote from the naughtiest of naughty songs. 'The Ball of Kirriemuir.' They had treated the story humorously as I guessed they and the rest of the press would treat this one about the posters.

### The Big Shike

An extra large number of people with notebooks and pencils at the ready were seen entering the Sheriff Court building and Matt and I watched with pleasure as one by one they enquired as to which room the Matt McGinn trial was to be held in. Matt had done a good job with the press, radio and television, contacting them by phone and on a personal basis in the two or three days prior to the trial.

The Sheriff before whom the trial was to take place proved to be a man with a sense of humour, and was ready with as many wisecracks as I, so that these journalists were to find their journey to the court worthwhile from the point of view of copy.

'With your permission, Milord, I should like to conduct my own defence,' said I and the Sheriff agreed that I should do so. The prosecutor called his first witness, Mister Cummings of the

Planning Department, who told how he had seen fifty one posters in various places throughout the city, how he had contacted me by telephone to warn me to get them down, how he had been in touch with the owners of the places on which the posters had been displayed and received letters from them stating that none of them had given Matt McGinn permission to display posters on their sites and these letters he produced to the court and read.

I asked Mister Cummings if he had ever seen me before, to which question he replied in the negative.

'Did you see me putting up these posters?' I asked and the Planning official replied, 'No.' The procurator intervened when I asked if Mister Cummings had seen any other posters displayed on these sites he had mentioned with other peoples' names on them.

'That is an irrelevancy, Milord,' said he.

'I would claim,' says I, 'that it is very relevant to part of my defence, which is that I have been singled out from thousands of people whose names are on posters throughout the city and I want to know why Teddy Taylor, Winifred Ewing, Gary Glitter, Glen Daly, Jimmy Reid, Billy Connolly and others have not been brought to court by the Planning Department.'

The Sheriff ruled against me but the pressmen's pencils were busy and they had some copy of which they would make use.

A younger man then took the stand to state that he had been an employee of the Planning Department and had been sent round the sites referred to and had seen the said posters which he described. I asked if he had been sent specifically to look for Matt McGinn posters and he replied in the affirmative. I then took the stand.

'Do you wish to take the oath?' the Sheriff asked. 'You do not have to, but naturally a great deal more weight will be placed upon your testimony if you do.' 'I am an atheist,' I replied, causing another ripple in the court as though I had just confessed to being a leper.

'Do you wish to affirm?' asked the judge.

'I do, Milord,' says I and I did swear to tell the truth and then proceeded to deny the charge that I had displayed the posters.

'Was this then the work of some good fairy?' asked the Sheriff.

'It's more likely to have been the work of some enemy of mine,' says I, 'causing me all this trouble and torment.'

The judge then pointed to the charge sheet and said with a

twinkle in his eye, 'Now what's this – "The Big Strike!"'

'No, it should be the Big Shike,' says I and the Sheriff and the others in the court burst forth with a gale of laughter.

'Order in court,' said the clerk, himself laughing as he spoke. His back to the Sheriff, he was unable to see that the judge himself was chuckling.

'And to what does that refer?' the judge asked.

'It's what they call sheiks in Saudi Arabia,' says I.

'And this here – "The Big Effen Bee!"' said the Sheriff. 'I don't have to ask what that is.'

'Effen,' says I, 'is a beautiful little town just outside Edinburgh, just nine hundred and forty miles outside Edinburgh. In fact, it is in France and it is famous for its honey so naturally there are a lot of bees there, not unnaturally known as the Effen Bees.'

With this the entire court with the exception of the Procurator Fiscal Depute, was caught in a kink of guffawing.

Under the relevant statute and specifically section 101 of the Town and Country Planning Act, 'It shall be deemed' that if your name is on a poster illegally displayed, then you are responsible and the judge said he felt he had no alternative but to fine me thirty pounds.

I could have pointed out that Woolworths, Boots and Emerald Gem Records were mentioned on the posters and therefore could have been similarly 'Deemed' to be responsible. But I was only too glad at the smallness of the fine. Ludicrously I could have been fined one hundred and sixty three thousand pounds under the Act which some civil servants and presumably half-drunken Members of Parliament had drafted and passed, laying it down that fines totalling two hundred pounds per poster plus ten pounds per day for each day the said poster remained affixed were liable.

Since these fifty one with my name on them had been up for three hundred days I would have been unable to pay the maximum fine and I suppose since I didn't have a bean I could have been forced to spend the remainder of my little life in Peterhead Prison.

Poor old Kilroy, whose name was daubed on millions of walls by other people throughout the world, had better watch out.

For myself, now, according to this ruling of the Court anyone who does not like me need only stick my name on a wall and 'It shall be deemed' I am responsible.

By Glasgow standards of the past Bain Street had been quite a good Street, but now the Calton area in which it was situated was crumbling under the combined efforts of natural decay and of the hammers and bouncing balls of Glasgow's demolishers who were having a bonanza smashing into smithereens the masonry, timbers and bricks of a couple of centuries and creating a dust to tickle the nostrils and lungs of the few old Caltonians who were intent upon sticking it out to the last. These consisted in the majority of solid, respectable and decent working class folk and a small minority of poorer souls who had been destroyed by a number of environmental factors and drink.

Moving on, I stopped to look at the street where I had been born.

I could envisage the two pubs at either end of the small street, the stable with the five horses, and the sixth horse which was kept in the room by another tenant in number fifteen. I could recall the zoo and the Unitarian church. I could see the sweetie shop and the sausage casings manufacturer's, the High Class Florist's and the women's model lodging house – Ross Street Home for Females. Oh those poor unfortunates; I could remember the Wee Fairy and Rhubarb Legs and Baldy Kate, the latter being recommended by sailors who had tasted women in every port in the world as the worst bedworker in the entire universe.

The memories flooded back of the Smiddy and the Joiner's and the smell of the Hamcurer's from which thick black smoke came belching down upon our houses.

Carefully picking my way among the debris of where the stable had been, I recollected the time when some of the local lads had broken into the same, had taken out the horses at one o'clock in the morning, mounted them and proceeded to race them up and down the Gallowgate shouting, 'Hi Ho Silver'.

I remembered the times when lads, their faces covered with rubber masks, would accost girls coming from Barrowland Dance Hall in the war years. Stepping out from the shadow of doorways, they would confront the poor young girls with 'Can I see you home' and such salutations. Then there were the occasions when they would stand in twos against dark walls; one on the inside pretending to be a female with their trousers rolled up to attract the 'knee creepers' who frequented the area looking for the 'bad women' from the model. Then there was the Dummy, the figure of a man they had made up which looked very much the real thing and with this they had engaged in very dangerous larks. There was a billiard hall in the Gallowgate, two stairs up, facing Charlotte Street and outside the window they would place this thing and as Barrowland was emptying of revellers – with or without lumbers or escorts – they would shout through the partly open window, 'stand out the road, I'm gonnie jump'. This created scenes of hysteria down below as crowds would make a huge circle and girls could be heard screaming, 'Don't throw yourself oot Mister.' 'Don't kill yersel.'

Into the circle they would in fact push the dummy and as people ran back in horror one of them would rush from the close below and pull the imitation body out of sight leaving the crowd to wonder whether the man was dead or alive.

On one particularly cruel occasion they had pushed the dummy under the front of a car which ran over it. The poor unfortunate driver left the car and sat down sick on the pavement for fully ten minutes before looking, only to find that whatever it was he had run over had been removed.

I brought to mind the faces of the five hundred or so who had lived there; mostly big families we were, and most of us connected by blood and marriage, the Logans connected to the Morrisons, connected to the McGonigles who were connected to the McMahons who were connected to the Armstrongs who were connected to the Robertsons who were connected to the Sloans who were cousins of ours.

The Buchanans who lived in number fifteen came to mind and it struck me that that was as good a justification as any for my wearing the Buchanan tartan bonnet I had on. If you have Buchanans living in your street you are entitled to wear a Buchanan tartan bonnet.

Scenes of childhood flooded through my brain and I could see a vast crowd of Orangemen rushing up the Street with policemen swinging batons.

The Orangemen had been particularly angered by the barber's pole at the corner, the red bits of it having been painted green overnight by the Dorises who had lived next door to us. I remembered a woman with a particularly bad gash on her shin

8 Ross Street, 1967.                                          Photograph by B. Shuel

which had been administered by the horse of a mounted policeman.

The Street itself was well known as being almost entirely inhabited by Catholics which had angered Mick McLatchie, who was not a true Mick but in fact a very devout Orangeman, and, who, in order to display his devotion to the cause of Prince William and the Protestant ascendancy had only a few months before slashed both his wrists, thereby gaining a promise from his only daughter Betty that she would not marry the Catholic boy with whom she had been tig-toying in spite of the fact that she was then six months pregnant to him. The same Mick had given up an apprenticeship in the printing trade the moment he heard he had to bring in a reference to the Father of the Chapel. On one occasion when he was being chided by a fellow Protestant on the possibility of one day having to lie beneath a couch of green grass, Mick had said, 'Not me, I'll arrange to be buried beneath the blue grass of Kentucky' and thereupon had a will made to that effect.

Mick found warmth in Ibrox where he never failed to turn up for a game involving his beloved Rangers and found solace in the Orange Lodges of the Clyde and very specially in Belfast on the

Twelfth of every July. There might be unpleasant things in the world, but to Mick it was a simple, uncomplex affair in which all the evils were attributable to the Vatican and the Priesthood. The Crimean, the Boer and the First and Second World Wars were the work of the Pope. Were not Hitler and Mussolini Catholics? Even Vietnam, was that not the work of Kennedy. Mick had it all there in his pamphlets which he garnered in the Lodges and in his mail from the Neat Little Town across the Irish Sea.

Yes, a stranger would have looked at Ross Street and seen two large and filthy-looking vacant lots, but I saw much, much more.

# Songs & Poems

# INDEX OF SONGS AND POEMS

# THE BALLAD OF JOHN MacLEAN

Chorus
*Dominie, Dominie,*
*There was nane like John MacLean,*
*The fighting Dominie.*

Tell me where ye're gaun, lad, and who ye're gaun to meet—
I'm headed for the station that's in Buchanan Street,
I'll join 200,000 that's there to meet the train
That's bringing back to Glasgow our own dear John MacLean:

Tell me whaur he's been, lad, and why has he been there?
They've had him in the prison for preaching in the Square,
For Johnny held a finger at all the ills he saw,
He was right side o' the people, but he was wrong side o' the law:

Johnny was a teacher in one o' Glasgow's schools
The golden law was silence but Johnny broke the rules,
For a world of social justice young Johnny couldnae wait,
He took his chalk and easel to the men at the shipyard gate.

The leaders o' the nation made money hand o'er fist
By grinding down the people by the fiddle and the twist,
Aided and abetted by the preacher and the Press—
John called for revolution and he called for nothing less:

The bosses and the judges united as one man
For Johnny was a danger to their '14-'18 plan,
They wanted men for slaughter in the fields of Armentiers,
John called upon the people to smash the profiteers:

They brought him to the courtroom in Edinburgh toun,
But still he didnae cower, he firmly held his ground,
And stoutly he defended his every word and deed,
Five years it was his sentence in the jail at Peterheid:

Seven months he lingered in prison misery
Till the people rose in fury, in Glasgow and Dundee,
Lloyd George and all his cronies were shaken to the core,
The prison gates were opened, and John was free once more:

© Heathside Music

# THE BALLAD OF THE Q4

The Mary and the Lizzie they were made right here
But you'll never see the likes of them I fear.
They were the finest on the silver sea.
They were built by the hands of men like me.

Chorus
*Thank you, Dad, for all your skill*
*But the Clyde is a river that'll no stand still.*
*You did gey well, but we'll do more.*
*Make way for the finest of them all, Q4.*

We have an order we'll fulfil
With a touch o' the master and a bit more skill.
Now the backroom boys are under way
And the pens will be rolling till the launching day.

There's Big Tom O'Hara with his burning gear
The plumber and the plater and the engineer
There's young Willie Wylie with his welding rod
They're waiting at the ready for the backroom nod.

We'll burn and cut and shape and bend
We'll be welding and riveting and in the end
When the painter's dabbed his final coat
We'll be launching the finest ever ship afloat.

We've worked and sweated and toiled and now
See the expert's hand from stern to bow
She's ready for the torments o' the sea
She's a credit to the Clyde and you and me.

# THE BEE FROM THE OLD TOWN OF EFFEN

*(Just outside Ecclefechan, just nine hundred and twenty two and a half miles outside Ecclefechan, in fact, in France lies the sleepy little town of EFFEN, the curative qualities of whose honey is renowned all over the civilised world – and in Glasgow. The very extraordinary bees who produce this honey are not unnaturally referred to as EFFEN Bees in and around the town whose quaint architecture is marred by the factory in its centre where half the population are employed in the manufacturing of Gendarmes' truncheons or, as the French choose to call them, policemen's batons.)*

He kept bees in the old town of Effen
An Effen beekeeper was he
And one day this Effen beekeeper
Was stung by a big Effen bee

Now this big Effen beekeeper's wee Effen wife
For the big Effen polis she ran
For there's nobody can sort out a big Effen bee
Like a big Effen polisman can

This big Effen polisman he did his nut
And he ran down the main Effen street
In his hand was a big Effen baton
He had big Effen boots on his feet

The polis got hold of this big Effen bee
And he twisted the Effen bee's wings
But this big Effen bee got his own back
For this big Effen bee had two stings

Now they're both in the Effen museum,
Where the Effen folk often come see
The remains of the big Effen polis
Stung to death by the big Effen bee

That's the end of that wee Effen story
'Tis an innocent wee Effen tale
But if you ever tell it in Effen
You'll end up in the old Effen jail

# BENNY LYNCH

Chorus
*The whole of the river sang 'Benny Has Been,*
*Benny Has Been, Benny Has Been'.*
*Down in the city, that never was mean,*
*We all sang 'Benny Has Been'.*

Up from the heart of the Gorbals he rose,
Don't tramp on his toes, for everyone knows,
From then on when we see the bend in your nose,
We'll all sing 'Benny Has Been'.

Down to the shows Benny went as a youth,
To fight in the booth, I'll tell you the truth,
Many's the big man was short of a tooth,
As he sang 'young Benny Has Been'.

To Manchester City young Benny went down,
To meet Jacky Brown, he picked up the crown.
He came back in triumph to old Glasgow town,
And the city sang 'Benny Has Been'.

He beat Small Montana, he floored Peter Kane,
Sent him back to train – then downed him again,
The Lynch-pin of boxing inflicted more pain,
And the city sang 'Benny Has Been'.

The city had T.B. the city had booze,
Her victims she'd choose, and send out the news,
That Benny would win, and then Benny would lose,
And the city sang 'Benny Has Been'.

# BIDDY McGRATH

Tune: *Mrs McGrath*

Well, have you heard of Biddy McGrath?
She strangled two sailors with the straps of her bra.
She tied one strap around the little fella's head,
And she threw him in the Liffey like a crust of bread.

Chorus
*With yer too-ri-a, fal-the-diddle-da,*
*Too-ri-oor-ri-oor-ri-a,*
*With yer too-ri-a, fal-the-diddle-da,*
*Too-ri-oor-ri-oor-ri-a.*

Biddy turned round on the big fella then,
She took him in her fingers like a ball-point pen,
She twirled him north and she twirled him south,
Then she tied the other strap around the poor fella's mouth.

The policeman said to Biddy McGrath,
'What's this you've been doing with the straps of your bra?'
Says she, 'Get along and on with yer job',
And she stuffed the remainder in the policeman's gob.

108

The judge he said to Biddy McGrath,
'Yer a thorough disgrace to yer ma and yer pa.'
Says she, 'Them sailors were feeding me the cure,
And treating me as if I were a lady.'

So if you're ever in Dublin Town,
Where Nelson's monument used to be found,
And you come across a girl with a brand new bra,
Beware if her name be Biddy McGrath.

# THE BIG ORANGE WHALE

Tune: *They say that the women are worse than the men*

A big orange whale came up the Clyde,
   *Rifol-rifol-tittyfolay*
A big orange whale came up the Clyde,
Landed in Ibrox on Saturday night,
   *With a rifolay-tittyfolay-rifol-rifol-tittyfolay.*

This bloody big whale climbed intae the park,
Where the players were trying to train in the dark,

The bloody big whale sat doon in the goal,
An' drove all the players hauf up the pole,

They went and they wakened their manager up,
'If we cannae get training we'll no win the cup,'

Said he: 'It's an answer tae all o' ma prayers',
An' he ran doon an' signed the whale up for the 'Gers,

With the whale for a goalie, they set oot tae win,
An' the other ten men just heidered them in,

They won every league an' they won every cup,
An' their average score was seventeen-up,

They were top o' the league for twenty-four years,
When the whale had to go, it left them in tears,

110

Tae give him the sack made them sad as could be,
Bit they'd caught him one Friday with fish for his tea,

They'd been in such a hurry tae sign the whale on,
They'd forgotten tae ask him: 'Whit school are ye from?',

Now the moral no doubt you'll think is a queer yin,
Rangers won't have a whale if it's not Presbyterian.

# BIG SAMMY

Tune: *Dick Derby the Cobbler*

I started work up in Partick,
But my workmates were acting gey queer
For everything I laid my hands on
These were the words I could hear:

Chorus
*'That thing belongs to Big Sammy,*
*The big fighting man of the toon,*
*If you touch it he nearly goes barmy,*
*So scram before Sammy comes roun'!'*

I spotted some tools in a corner,
I lifted a shovel and pick,
Says a hulking big six-foot-two brickie:
'For heaven's sake lay them down quick!'

I went for some tea when the break came,
I walked in and lifted a cup,
The can boy near fell o'er the fire
And squealed like a six weeks' old pup:

I lifted a stool and I held it,
Says I: 'Where does big Sammy stay?
I don't care how big is Big Sammy,
I'll soon sort him out the day!'
I broke in and asleep by the fire
Was a man that weighed 34 stone,
With a stool in my hand I attacked him,
Says I: 'I'll soon stop them that moan:'

He slept all the while I attacked him,
My muscular strength was all gone,
When a woman rushed in and she's screaming:
'Would you not leave the poor child alone?'

Chorus
*'That child belongs to Big Sammy
The big fighting man of the toon,
If you touch it he nearly goes barmy,
So scram before Sammy comes roun'!'*

© Heathside Music

# BIG WILLIE'S BLUES

Tune: *St. James' Infirmary Blues*

I went up to the Royal Infirmary, to see Big Willie there,
I stepped up to his bedside and sat down on his chair.

He didn't look too cheerful, his face was turning blue.
I asked him how his health was, but all that Willie said was 'Oooooh . . .'

I spoke to him about racing, football and politics too,
I asked his opinion of the weather, but all that Willie said was 'Oooooh . . .'

From the table he snatched up a notebook, from my pocket he picked out a
He began to scribble something and he lay down peacefully then.

The sister she came running, she said Big Willie was dead,
I pointed to that paper, I said 'Those are the last words he said.'

The sister read that message, and I found I'd made a boob,
It said 'Ya stupid lookin' clown ye, you're sittin' on ma oxygen tube.'

© Heathside Music

113

# BINGO BELLA

Tune: *The darktown strutters' ball*

I'll be down to collect you for the bingo, Bella,
Rendezvous in the Gallowgate,
Mind, Bella, don't be late
    We've got to be there before the crowd starts queuing.
Remember when we get there, Bella,
We're gonnie be trying for the big snowball,
But whether it's win or lose,   -
We'll have a damn good feed of the booze,
    Tomorrow night at the South Side Bingo Ball.

You and I were nearly winning last time, Bella,
If it hadn't been for Maggie McGill,
Wouldn't yon one make you ill?
    Seven hundred and twenty two smackers.
Hasn't spoken to a neighbour since then
After tapping them for seventeen years
Ah but, mind you, there's one thing nice,
Lightning never strikes the same place twice,
    So we will have a chance at the South Side Bingo Ball.

We'll be catching the bus to the bingo, Bella,
We will alight at the Gorbals Cross,
Pie and peas with tomato sauce,
    Till we can lay our hands on that snowball.
Then we'll be heading for the taxi, Bella,
To the Rogano wi' yer ten bob tip,
And when they ask us what we want,
We'll say pour us oot yer creme du mint
    Tomorrow night at the South Side Bingo Ball.

# THE BUTCHERS OF GLASGOW

The butchers of Glasgow have all got their pride
But they'll tell you that Willie's the prince
For Willie the butcher he slaughtered his wife
And he sold her for mutton and mince.

It's a terrible story to have to be telt
And a terrible thing to be done
For what kind of man is it slaughters his wife
And sells her a shilling a pun.

For lifting his knife and ending her life
And hanging her high like a sheep
You widnae object but you widnae expect
He wid sell the poor woman so cheap.

But the Gallowgate folk were delighted
It didnae cause them any tears
They swore that Willie's wife Mary
Was the best meat he'd sold them in years.

# CAN O' TEA

Chorus
*The champagne flows, the wine glass glows.*
*The shipyard gates'll have to close.*
*They say it's all because of me.*
*And I cannae hae my can o' tea.*
*Dowra ya the day my can o' tea.*

For forty years and fourteen mair
The men that work with Donald Blair
They've aye had a middle of the morning plan
They stop at ten to boil their can.

But Donald he was awful wise
Although he always closed his eyes
He never ever gie'd us leave
So he'd a trump card up his sleeve

This morning Donald came to me
He pointed to my can o' tea
Then he let out an awful roar
Said he 'Young man get out that door'

But the men said I'd been victimised
For the Union I had organised
So when I laid down my can o' tea
A thousand men marched out wi' me.

116

# COORIE DOON

Chorus
*Coorie Doon, Coorie Doon, Coorie Doon, my darling,*
*Coorie Doon the day.*

Lie doon, my dear, and in your ear,
To help you close your eye,
I'll sing a song, a slumber song,
A miner's lullaby.

Your daddy's doon the mine my darling,
Doon in the Curlby Main,
Your daddy's howking coal my darling.
For his own wee wean.

There's darkness doon the mine my darling,
Darkness, dust and damp.
But we must have oor heat, oor light,
Oor fire and oor lamp.

Your daddy coories doon my darling,
Doon in a three foot seam,
So you can coorie doon my darling,
Coorie doon and dream.

# DEPTH OF MY EGO

Chorus
*Deep in my heart and deep in my mind*
*Deep in the depth of my ego*
*Deep in my breast lies a treasure chest*
*A world that only I can know*

You can criticise me try to analyse me
Put me in your little pigeon hole
But I'll still hold the key to the place where I am free
A place that only I control.

I can love you dearly I can love you true
I can love you long and love you well
But I must have my own song only I can sing
My own tale that only I can tell

Place me in your prison put me in your cell
Lock me up and throw away the key
I will only wander wander all around
This big world that's inside me.

# THE DUNDEE GHOST

Now a dead man seldom walks and he very rarely talks,
It's no' very often you'll find him runnin' aroon',
But I'm a refugee frae a graveyard in Dundee,
And I've come to haunt some hooses in Glesca' toon.
Ooh, Ooh! And I've come to haunt some hooses in Glesca' toon.

The reason I arose was to get masel' some clothes,
For it really gets hanguva cold below the grund.
But I whispered to myself, Ach, I think I might as well
Hang around for a while and ha'e some fun.
Ooh, Ooh! Hang around for a while and ha'e some fun.

A man put out his light on a cauld and windy night,
I showed him one o' my eyes and slapped his heid.
He says, 'Oh,' and I says, 'Boo.' He says, 'Who the heck are you?'
I says, 'Don't be feart; I'm only a man that's deid.'
Ooh, Ooh! I says,'Don't be feart; I'm only a man that's deid.'

The fella knelt and prayed, and this was what he said—
'Why in the name of God ha'e ye picked on me?'
I pulled away his rug and I skelpt him on the lug;
'The reason,' I says, 'I'll very soon let you see.'
Ooh, Ooh! 'The reason,' I says, 'I'll very soon let you see.'

When he brought the polis in I battered him on the chin.
The polis turned aroond and blamed my friend.
He marched him to the jail. He'll be in there quite a while,
But I'll see naebody's taken his single-end.
Ooh, Ooh! But I'll see naebody's taken his single-end.

Now, the polis thought him daft, and a lot of people laughed,
When the fella said a ghost was in his hoose.
But what the fella said was true, and I might be visiting you,
So just remember I'm still on the loose.
Ooh, Ooh! So just remember I'm still on the loose.

# ETERNITY WOULD SOON BE OVER

Chorus
*Eternity would soon be over*
*If I could spend it with my love.*

Each day I spend, my love, without you,
Each long, long day is as a year,
Each smile I smile with arms about you,
When you are gone becomes a tear.

When Autumn brings her gentle breeze in,
I count each leaf when I'm alone,
But I count no leaf, I count no season,
When the lips I love are on my own.

So come my love, these arms are waiting,
To enfold my sole delight,
Send my joys all escalating,
And put these lonely hours to flight.

© Heathside Music

# THE FOOTBA' REFEREE

Chorus
*Why did I ever become a football referee?*
*I could have been an engineer or a sailor on the sea.*
*Wherever there's a fault to find they always pick on me.*
*Why did I ever become a football referee?*

I used to play at centre half when I was very young,
In speaking out for fair play I never could hold my tongue.
The men at the top were watching and they quickly spotted me.
They says, 'Now there is a decent man, we'll make him a referee.'

When first I took my whistle out I did feel very proud,
I played it like a fluter and I smiled at all the crowd,
I gave them two decisions and I heard a terrible boo,
Then fifty-thousand voices roared 'Coconuts to you'!

When Rangers played the Celtic, I was stuck out on the field,
I'd only been there a minute or two when the crowd began to squeal.
The half o' them said 'He's a Fenian fae the heart o' Ireland.'
The others said, 'He's a bluenose and he's there by the shake o' the hand.'

The game had gone on half-an-hour when two began to fight
I tried to separate them and to tell them who was right.
They bashed me and they battered me and they left me nearly lame,
The crowd a' roared out, 'Bury him! and let's get on with the game.'

They brought me out to Italy as a very honoured guest,
Between Milan and Roma, I did my level best.
But the crowd they didna fancy me — I could tell by the way they spieled.
They hired a helicopter to take me oot o' the field.

121

# THE FOREMAN O'ROURKE

It's maybe I'm right, and maybe I'm wrong,
Maybe I shouldnae go singing this song;
For the jury decided, and you may as well,
That a fellow like me should be roasting in Hell.

Chorus
*Hooch-aye, hooch till I fa'.*
*Hooch-aye, hooch till I dee.*

I had a gaffer, his name was O'Rourke.
He had a terrible passion for work;
In miles and in tons he took a' he could see,
But he never was greedy - he gied it tae me!

One day in the work I went roon for a smoke,
The door burst open, and there stood O'Rourke:
He started tae swear and he gied me his curse,
He insulted my mother, and that was far worse.

He jumped at my throat and it gave me a fright,
I was quick on my feet, and I stepped tae the right.
There was nothin' could stop him, this terrible man,
Till he landed feet up, wi' his heid in the pan.

I was trembling wi' fear when his heid gave a thud,
And I looked doon and saw that his claes were a' mud.
Yet it wisnae his claes were the worst o' his plight,
For his heid was jammed in there – a sorrowful sight.

I looked and I thought as I buckled my belt,
And you never could feel the compassion I felt:
'I'll wash a' his claes,' were the words that I said,
'Ach, and while I'm aboot it, I'll wash the man's heid.'

In Barlinnie I wait for the man tae come roon,
That'll open the door and let me drap doon.
And I'll pray for O'Rourke as they gie me the tug,
For they hang me the morra - for pullin' the plug.

© 1964 Harmony Music Ltd.

122

# THE GALLOWGATE CALYPSO

Chorus
*Maggie, Nelly and Mary Ann, Lizzie, Willie and Phil McCann*
*Get your jacket and don't be late: 'Murder, polis, in the Gallowgate.'*

In the Gallowgate on a Friday night
Folk a' gathered to see the sight
They came for miles and miles aroon
Ten o'clock when the pubs shut doon.

Time up bells began to ring
Then the barmen began to fling
Big souls, wee souls every kind
A' stoned drunk wi' the cheap red wine.

First man oot was big Shug Grant
'Up the Celtic' was his chant
He roars that oot just to show who's boss
He shouts 'Up Rangers' at Brigton Cross.

Blackpool May came oot and ran
Followed by a wee fat man
If he catches her she'll surely choke
She drank his wine then she picked his poke.

Danny Owens comes oot to fight
Threatens every man in sight
He trips and fa's and he's oot the game
His wife'll murder him when he gets hame.

Two big polis are the next we see
'Eat the Moose' and 'John the B'
Into the public hoose they ran
Late night drink wi' the publican.

# GET UP GET OUT

Chorus
*Get up get out ya lazy lout*
*Get intae your working claes.*
*Up to your knees in oil and grease*
*And do what your gaffer says.*

When I was young and short of tongue
A silly wee fool was I.
The morning after I left the school
I heard my mother cry—

I bought a clock, a rare wee clock,
So I could tell the time,
It wakened me every mornin'
With a very poetic rhyme.

I married a lass, a bonnie wee lass,
And kept her many a year,
But come what may she'd start the day,
By whispering in my ear.

There's some can lie as long as they like,
They're luckier men than me,
For I know I'll never get lying long,
I'm only five foot three.

# THE GLASGOW OLYMPICS

Tune: *Michael Row the Boat Ashore*

Fun and Games in Glasgow Town Hallelujah
The Olympic Games are coming round Hallelujah

In the Glasgow Green the hundred metres Hallelujah
In the Saracen Heid the hundred litres Hallelujah

In the long jump contest we'll go far Hallelujah
We'll hold them outside Betty's Bar Hallelujah

Security wise things should go sweet Hallelujah
We'll send in the Tongs and the Maryhill Fleet Hallelujah

We'll set an example to Holland and France Hallelujah
In religious tolerance Hallelujah

In new games we'll produce some brammers Hallelujah
Catching the javelin and heiderin' the hammers Hallelujah

The boxing contests should prove fair Hallelujah
A square go here and a square go there Hallelujah

# HI JACK

Chorus
'Hi Jack' the navigator greeted me,
'Hi Jack' the pilot said the same,
'Hi Jack' – the friendly way they treated me,
I simply couldn't wait to get aboard that plane.

London to Glasgow isn't very far at all,
But I was in a hurry, I decided I would fly,
But from the very moment I got into the booking hall
The only thing that I could hear was 'Hi'.

'I hope' says I to a lady in a mackintosh
'When we get to Glasgow the weather isn't bleak.
Says she 'Have a word with the long range weatherman,
You won't be seeing Glasgow any time this week.' She says:

'Hi Jack, we're turning left at Birmingham.
Hi Jack.' She was speaking very plain.
'Sorry' says she 'if it causes any bother,
But I have a date in Cuba with the sugar cane.'

Fidel Castro met us in Havana,
Fidel couldn't have been nicer to a toff.
Rum and coffee and a lovely big banana,
Then quick as a flick he gave us a kick and says 'Buzz off.'

'Right' says the pilot, 'we're on our way to Glasgow,
By this evening you'll be sitting in your home.'
But these kind words were quickly contradicted
By a North American gent with a home-made bomb.

*Hi Jack, we landed in Miami,*
*I could hear Sammy Davis Jr sing.*
*Hi Jack, we took aboard a laundryman,*
*But he could only say 'Hi Jack Peking.'*

From Peking we travelled on to Moscow
At the request of a commissar.
There we met a little Orangeman
Who wanted to go to Belfast but he had no car.

From Belfast we then moved on to Dublin,
We arrived there just the other day.
Now they've told us they're sending us to Israel
Unless we sign as members of the IRA.

# THE HIELAN'MAN

Ten thousand Roman sodgers
To the Hielans they came North.
And they had conquered millions
Frae the Tiber tae the Forth.
They landed near Loch Lomond
For the night they thought they'd lie,
But frae somewhere on the Cobbler Hill,
They heard this terrible cry.

Chorus
*Gregali, Gregaloo!*
*Come up and fight ya cowardly crew,*
*I'll have you for my pot of stew;*
*You're feart tae fight wi' me!*

On top was a bearded Hielan'man
Wi' a kilt and a big claymore;
He looked a bit ferocious
So old Caesar sent up four.
Then he sat doon tae supper
By the bright light o' the moon,
But he lost his taste for vino
When four heids came rollin' doon.

Then he sent up Mark Anthony
Wi' another fifty-five:
'Go bring tae me that rascal's heid,
Or I'll have ye skinned alive!'
They heard a clash o' metal then
Until the night was done;
But then there came this terrible cry
Wi' the risin' o' the sun.

He next sent up a thousand men
This Hielan'man tae crack;
But oot o' a' that thousand
There was only one came back.
'O Caesar,' screamed the sodger
Wi' his heid a' black and blue,
'That rascal has been kiddin' us,
There's not just one – but two!'

So Caesar picked his suitcase up
And he ran southwards then.
He was doin' eighty miles an hour
But he couldnae catch his men.
Now maybe you will wonder
Why I've told this tale at all;
Well, it has a simple moral
And they call it –
        HADRIAN'S WALL!

E

# I HAE SEEN THE HIELANDS

I was born in dear old Glasgow, in a Gallowgate tenement,
When people spoke of my bonny land I didn't know what they meant.
But then I took to travel, I moved far and wide,
Now when I speak of my native land I speak with loving pride:
*For I hae seen the Hielands, I hae seen the Low,*
*And I will brag o' my native land wherever I may go.*

Old Nature took a tantrum, many's the age gone by,
To outdo all of her wondrous works she thought she'd hae a try,
She toiled and she thundered, she rumbled and she rolled,
She made the Hielands o' Scotland then she threw away the mould:

Come rambling up by Oban, strolling down by Perth,
In the rugged hills o' Argyllshire find the sweetest place on earth;
Go gazing by the Cuillins, see the Lomond in the mist,
In the lovely island of Moula hear the songbird at its best:

The Irish and the English, the African and Turk,
For a world of joy and harmony together we will work.
On the shore of foreign brothers we'll lay no robber's hand,
And all we wish is to toil and work in our own native land:

# I OWE YOU

Chorus
*For an I owe I owe I owe you
I owe you I owe you
For an I owe I owe I owe you
An I owe I owe you.*

An H.P. man frae Polmadie came to me frae Polmadie,
An H.P. man he pestered me for an I.O., I.O.U.
Says he, 'Ye'll want a motor car. Jaguar? Right you are.
I'll give you yer motor car, give me yer I.O.U.'

Insurance man frae Cambuslang, came along frae Cambuslang.
Says he, 'In case yer car goes wrang give me yer I.O.U.'
A garage man in Burnbank, filled my tank, in Burnbank,
Now he has got me tae thank for an I.O., I.O.U.

On that car I've travelled far, tae Dunbar, Balmaha,
Now I'm off tae Arrochar on an I.O., I.O.U.
A police car is chasing me, racing me, chasing me,
An' if they should catch up with me, they'll take me nae I.O.U.

# THE IBROX DISASTER

New Year bells had been ringing,
All Scotland was singing,
The old year had died, and the new had been born,
As the news of disaster, from Ibrox came spreading,
The news that would cause a whole nation to mourn.

Two great goals had been scored, in the last dying moments,
Jimmy Johnstone for Celtic, for Rangers young Stein,
Their supporters all cheered them with voices of thunder,
Unknowing what waited on staircase thirteen.

Sixty six people died, some in flower of their manhood,
When the fences gave way, and the barriers bent,
Seasoned Glasgow policemen, their faces all tear-stained,
With brave efforts endeavoured, far worse to prevent.

All of Glasgow enjoined for the first time in history,
In the Glasgow Cathedral, no Billy, no Dan,
But the Old Firm united, to pray for the victims,
Of a tragedy set in the memory of man.

New Year bells had been ringing, all Scotland was singing,
The old year had died and the new had been born.
As the news of disaster from Ibrox came spreading,
The news that would cause a whole nation to mourn.

# IF IT WISNAE FOR THE UNION

Chorus
*Too ra loo ra loo ra loo*
*I'll tell ye something awfu' true,*
*Ye wouldna' hae your telly the noo,*
*If it wisnae for the Union.*

I had a boss in Aberdeen,
The nicest fella ever I've seen,
But I think he thought I wis awfa green,
Afore I joined the Union.

I had a boss they called Colquhoun
The nicest fella in Glesga Toon.
Except for keeping yer wages doon,
Afore we joined the Union.

I had a boss his name wis Black,
He told me I could call him Jack,
He wis helluva good at gi'en ye the sack,
Afore we joined the Union.

Too-ra-loo-ra-loo-ra-loo,
I'll tell you something else that's true,
The boss would hae us black and blue,
If it wisnae for the Union.

I had a lass in Inverness,
And she wis one o' the very best,
But we couldnae afford tae marry unless
I went and joined the Union.

Too-ra-loo-ra-loo-ra-loo,
There's twenty four hours in a day it's true,
And we'd ha' worked the twenty two,
If it wisnae for the Union.

Men and women listen tae me,
It's time tae rise up aff yer knee,
So raise the flag of Unity,
And forward with the Union.

# I'M LOOKING FOR A JOB

Chorus
*I'm looking for a job with a sky-high pay,*
*A four-day week and a two-hour day,*
*S'maybe it's because I'm inclined that way*
*But I never did like being idle!*

I don't want glory and I don't want fame,
I left school with a modest aim,
I went to the Labour Exchange for work,
Here is what I sang to the wee broo clerk:

Now that, says he, is a rare wee song,
To come frae a lad so big and strong,
Through the door on the left and take this card:
You can sing to the gaffer down in Harland's yard:

I sang it to the gaffer but he thought me daft,
I've never even heard such a horse's laugh,
He gathered around him all his men,
And as one big choir, they sang then:

Their voices rang o'er the riverside,
And it became the song of the Clyde,
Its words were heard the whole world round,
And it was known as the Clydeside Sound:

© Heathside Music

134

# I'VE PACKED UP MY BAGS

Chorus
*I've packed up my bags, I must go,*
*Far away from the town of Glasgow,*
*I'm headed for Swindon or maybe for London,*
*In search of a living I'll go.*

My name it is Patrick McPhee, and the Gallowgate folk all know me,
'Tis there I'd have lingered, but I was glue-fingered,
And landed up in Barlinnie.
The reason that I had to fall, I stole from a man they call Gall,
I thought it was queer that he had so much gear
While I hadn't any at all:

I went from Barlinnie today to the Labour Exchange right away,
I said to the clerk I was looking for work
With half decent hours and good pay.
Said he: 'You might find it quite hard,' and I saw what he wrote on my card,
'From that day to this'n' McPhee's been in prison'
And that simply meant I was barred:

A girl before I went inside, I'd promised to make her a bride,
But she wouldn't wait at the Barlinnie gate
For that was so undignified.
So now I'm a poor man but free, though headed far away I must be,
Where I'll find a living, though there's no forgiving
A man that's been in Barlinnie:

© 1966 Harmony Music Ltd.

# JANETTA

Music adapted traditional Irish

Moonshine on me
As I sit by the surging sea
Alone
Knowing you are gone
To embrace me never

Throbbing the sands
Beneath my hands as the wind blows
Bringing no solace
To the ache my heart knows

And yet and yet
As since we met
I still love you
Of all womankind
Never one above you

Sunshine on me
Come the dawn
Life must still go on
Come time
In your peerless role
Heal the wounds between us

From caverns of mind
Then will the bright gems come fleeing
Dear sweet thoughts of you
Will be daylight seeing

Moonshine on me.

# JEANNIE GALLACHER

Chorus
*With a fond embrace, a kiss upon her face,*
*A gentle hand upon her shoulder,*
*I sat her doon by the light o' the moon,*
*Many were the lies I told her.*

Now Jeannie Gallacher I am very fond of her,
In my arms I like to hold her.
I'm thankful today for the very special way
Nature did decide to mould her.

When the sun lies doon to accommodate the moon
And the evening breeze blows kindly,
Where the coal smoke comes fae the roon rid lums,
It's there wi' Jean ye'll find me.

And now the clock's made gains and we have so many weans,
Their names I never can recall,
Still Jeannie's fair, none the worse o' a' the wear,
And I love the lassie none the less at all.

When the race is run and the prizes have been won
And the poor old bones grow colder,
Jeannie Gallacher and I you may leave us down to lie,
So for a long time I may hold her.

# JENNY A' THINGS

Chorus
*Jenny A' Things*
*Jenny A' Things*
*Wish I had wings to fly*
*To my sweet Jenny*
*Jenny A' Things*
*Jenny A' Things*

On this man made island
Fishing for oil
And working for Jenny

Wish it were milder
Couldn't be wilder
Working for Jenny
Sweet Jenny A' Things

Wrestling with Neptune
But I will be home soon
Working for Jenny
Sweet Jenny A' Things

Storm winds are chillin
Diving and drilling
Working for Jenny
Sweet Jenny A' Things

# LIFE IS A FOUNTAIN

Chorus
*Life is a fountain, fast and free,*
*Love is a mountain, rolling to the sea,*
*Sip of the fountain, waters so rare,*
*Climb that mountain just because it's there.*
*La-la-la-la-la-, la-la-la-la-la,*
*La-la-la-la-la, la-la.*

Sitting by a fountain, fast and free,
By the side of a mountain rolling to the sea,
Two little birds were singing up above,
Telling us the meaning of life and love.

The waters of the fountain flow so fast,
I sit and I wonder how they can last,
They flow with the noon-day, dusk and the dawn,
They will be flowing when we're gone.

The ways of the mountain, nobody knows,
But one way is open when another one close,
Don't ask why, don't ask where,
Climb that mountain, just because it's there.

# THE LITTLE CARPENTER

Chorus
*He took a hammer and a nail and a little piece of wood,*
*He made a little table and a chair.*
*People heard his name, everybody came*
*To see the little carpenter.*

Joshua ben Joseph was a charming little boy,
His father gave him a joiner's set, he loved that little toy,
People came from miles around, then they popped their eyes;
For the lovely little boy with the tricky little toy started to philosophise.

He said feed the hungry, tend the sick and low,
Be Samaritan to the beggarman, share out all your gold;
Turn the cheek and be mild and meek, have love for every man,
Be he pink or rosy red, or yellow, black or tan.

Joshua ben Joseph to the temple went one day,
He sent the money-changing men upon their merry way;
But Joshua had gone too far for the men of power and gold:
In unity with the Pharisee, they said what we have we hold.

Final Chorus
*They took a hammer and a nail and a little piece of wood,*
*They hanged him then and there.*
*People heard his name, everybody came*
*To see the little carpenter.*

© Mozart Allan

# LITTLE TICKS OF TIME

Chorus
*Those little ticks of time keep on tocking, tocking, tocking,*
*Tick-a-tick-a-tick-tick-tocking all the day,*
*But those little ticks of time know no reason know no rhyme,*
*They just tick-a-tick-a-tick-tick-tock the time away.*

The sun picks up little drops of water
From the sea as she rolls around the sky.
When her hands are full endowed she makes a little cloud
And sends the little cloud drifting by.

The little cloud goes drifting through the heavens,
He has a little task he must fulfill.
He makes little water balls and gently lets them fall
As raindrops down upon the hill.

As the raindrops fall upon the hilltop,
Each one stops to say hello,
And their faces fairly beam as they make a little stream
And the little stream goes trickling down below.

The stream meets another and another,
And they come upon another running free,
And they gurgle as they run and all become as one ·
Mighty river flowing to the sea.

# LOTS OF LITTLE SOLDIERS

Tune: *The Jolly Beggarman*

My name is 'What you may call me' and my father's was as well
Of a little game he taught me now the story I will tell
We had lots of little soldiers and as sure as the day would come
I sent them into battle with the rattle of my drum.

Chorus
*I put them upon the table and I marched them all around*
*Then I battered them with the cannonballs and watched them falling down*
*I had lots of little crosses that I laid upon the dead*
*Then I patched up all the wounded ones and I sent them home to bed.*

I went round and asked the neighbours for a nickel or a dime
To help me buy some soldiers just to help me pass the time
They were always very kindly in supplying me with guns
And some of them even let me play at soldiers with their sons.

Whenever I went to the shop to buy my guns and tanks
The man there always smiled and patted me head and whispered 'Thanks.
If it wasn't for your soldier game I don' know what I'd do
You keep my business busy son so here's an extra few.'

144

One day I bought some aeroplanes but here was what I found
When I sent them in with bombs to help my army on the ground
They bombed up every soldier there and proved a sorrowful flop
I had to buy another hundred crosses from the shop.

I would very much like if I could teach this little game of guns
To my seven beautiful daughters and my fourteen lovely sons
But the man in the shop he gave me down a bomb from off the shelf
It blew up every soldier, all my neighbours and myself.

145

# MAGIC SHADOW SHOW

Chorus
*In and out, above, below*
*Phantom figures come and go,*
*Just a magic shadow show,*
*Come, love, watch with me.*

It may be sad, it may be fun,
The leaves of life fall one by one,
The wine of life too soon is done
In this magic shadow show.

A loaf of bread and you and me,
A jug of wine beneath the tree,
We will sit and we will see
A magic shadow show.

A thousand blossoms of today
Will soon be scattered into clay,
Today becomes a yesterday –
Magic shadow show.

Leave tomorrow and yesterday,
With old Khayyam come sip today,
Listen to my Rubaiyat,
Magic shadow show.

Could you and I with fate conspire,
Remould this scheme of things entire,
Nearer to the heart's desire,
What a magic shadow show.

# MAMBO

Mambo was a dusky man. The sun had burned him brown.
But when he met with the colour bar it never got him down.
He'd ask them what colour is the good Lord's skin
Tell me brother do
Is he black or is he brown or is he just like you?

He went into a bar one night but he heard the barman say
'We don't want no coloureds here,' so Mambo then said:
Pray tell me what colour is the good Lord's skin
Tell me brother do
Is he black or is he brown or is he just like you?

He went to pray in Pretoria but the preacher's face turned blue
He thumped on his bible and he told Mambo
'You're sitting in the White Man's pew,'
Oh tell me what colour is the good Lord's skin
Tell me brother do
Is he black or is he brown or is he just like you?

He went in search of a room one day but the landlord turned him down
Saying 'You can bet we've a room to let but man your skin is brown,
Oh tell me what colour is the good Lord's skin
Tell me brother do
Is he black or is he brown or is he just like you?

# MANURA MANYA

Tune: *The Kerry Recruit*

I have heard men complain o' the job that they're daein',
While they're howkin' the coal or they're diggin' the drain
But whatever they are, there is none can compar'
Wi' the man that stauns shovellin' manura man-ya.

Chorus
*Wi' manura man-ya, wi manura man-ya,*
*Wi' manura, manura, manura man-ya.*

Noo the streets o' the toon were a' covered aroon
Wi' stuff that wis colourful – golden and broon.
It was pit there, of course, by a big Clydesdale horse,
And they called it manura-manura, man-ya.

Noo I followed its track, wi' a shovel and sack,
And as often as not wi' a pain in my back.
It was a' for the rent, and the wonderful scent
O' manura, manura, manura-man-ya.

Noo I'm feelin' gey sour, for my job's been ta'en ower,
And everything noo is mechanical power:
And the roses that grow have nae odour oh no! –
Nae manura, manura, manura-man-ya.

148

# MORNING ELEANORA

Morning Eleanora, beautiful morning, beautiful morning.
Morning Eleanora, beautiful morning, beautiful day.
Time to rise frae bed and shake your sleepy head
An' then you'll have to be fed but it's such a lovely day.
Morning Eleanora, beautiful morning, beautiful morning.
Morning Eleanora, beautiful morning, beautiful day.

The honey bee is busy, beautiful morning, beautiful morning.
Honey bee is busy, beautiful morning, beautiful day.
He's hanging around the bowers, and he'll be there for hours.
Kissing all the flowers for it's such a lovely day.
Morning Eleanora, beautiful morning, beautiful morning.
Morning Eleanora, beautiful morning, beautiful day.

The birdie in the tree sings, beautiful morning, beautiful morning.
Birdie in the tree sings, beautiful morning, beautiful day.
The little yellow breast is cleaning up his nest.
He wants to look his best for it's such a lovely day.
Morning Eleanora, beautiful morning, beautiful morning.
Morning Eleanora, beautiful morning, beautiful day.

# MY FAITHER WAS BORN A HEBREW

Chorus
*My faither was born a Hebrew*
*My faither was born a Jew*
*My faither was born a Hebrew*
*And I am a Hebrew too*

It is five thousand years
Since my faither's folk all fled
In search of milk and honey
And by Moses they were led

Now Jesus was a preacher
He was heard by quite a few
But when he was going around the place
They said 'He's just a Jew'.

A lauddie needs his lassie
A lassie needs her laud
But they didna understand
Till they sent for Sigmund Freud

The workers worked in dungeons
They didna have a pal
But then along comes Charlie
And he writes Das Kapital

The atom was a tiny thing
The scientists all knew
Along comes Abey Einstein
And splits the thing in two

There's good and bad in Scotia
There's good in Timbuktu
There's good and bad in every lad
So dinnae run doon the Jew

© 1964 Harmony Music Ltd.

# ON THE ROAD FROM ALDERMASTON

On the road from Aldermaston on an Easter Sunday morn
A hundred thousand marchers moved in the face of jeer and scorn
From Inverness and London town, from Pakistan and Greece,
And their badge was the badge of the C.N.D., their cause the cause of peace.

The sun rose high that morning to guide us on our way,
And as we looked high on his smiling eye these words I heard him say,
'For far too long I've been hid from view by dark and thunderous clouds,
But now I can shine on this daughter of mine with her singing, surging crow

I'll lead you to Trafalgar and I'll lead you further still,
To a world of peace and harmony where none shall want to kill,
Where the mother Earth I've given you will be your pride and joy,
And where none in pursuit of the golden gain will wish her to destroy.'

On the road from Aldermaston on an Easter Sunday morn
A hundred thousand marchers moved in the face of jeer and scorn
From Inverness and London town, from Pakistan and Greece,
And their badge was the badge of the C.N.D., their cause the cause of peace.

# THE PILL

Tune: *Kissin' in the Dark*

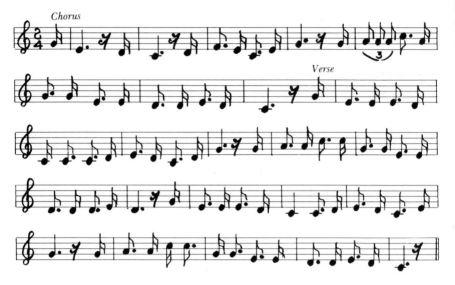

Chorus
*The Pill, the Pill, I'm pining for the Pill,*
*I'll never have any more because they're going to bless the Pill.*

I wed when I was seventeen,
I hadn't many brains;
Says I the very thing to do
Is fill the hoose wi' weans.
But when I got the room full
I went to see the priest,
To tell him my man Willie
Was behaving like a beast:

He gave me such a terrible row
My eyes were filled wi' tears:
'How long have you been wed?' says he,
Says I, 'This seven years.'
Says he, 'You'd better give over
All your evil sinful tricks –
You've been married seven years
And you've only got the six!'

I'm coming up for forty,
In my faith I've aye been true;
The very last time I tallied them
I counted twenty-two.
But now I've lost the notion
For we're running short o' names,
Though Willie he would welcome more –
He's fond o' havin' weans:

Now they're talking of the Pill
They've filled my heart wi' hope.
I'm sitting here and waiting
On a signal frae the Pope.
I went along tae buy some
At fifteen-bob a tin –
I hope we hae the Pope's O.K.
Before my man comes in!

# POLLY HAD A POODLE

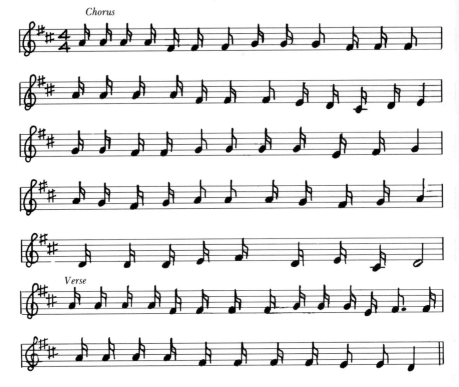

Chorus
*Polly had a poodle-o, poodle-o, poodle-o,*
*Polly had a poodle-o, piddled all the day.*
*Piddled on the carpet, piddled on the chair,*
*Piddled on the sofa, piddled on the flair.*
*Polly's poodle piddled all the day.*

Polly brought the polis in to give the dog a boot.
When he came in the doggie had a wee run oot.

They took him out to India, there they let him out.
Since the day he got there they've never had a drought.

The farmers all around had a very heavy yield,
They hired Polly's poodle to irrigate their fields.

He followed all the football, he knew all the rules,
He never missed a post when he was daen the pools.

# RAP TAP TAP

Chorus
*Rap, tap, tap, upon yer finger,*
*Rap, tap, tap, upon yer palm,*
*Rap, tap, tap, upon yer hand,*
*And I'll leave you with a blister like a Belfast ham.*

Before I ever took to teaching I was a fairly decent chap,
Then they gave me fifty weans and a lovely length o' leather strap.

'Och!' says I, 'I'll never use it, weans can all respond to talk,'
I told them that, then turned aroond and a boy let fly a cake of chalk.

'The boy that threw that chalk,' says I 'He'll never grow tae be a man,
He's far too feart tae show himself.' But he did, and he threw another one.

To strap a boy's an awfy business, every one's a mother's son,
Take the straps frae a' the teachers – issue everyone a gun.

# THE RED YO YO

Wee Ann took her Yo-Yo, tae school she did go, though
She shouldnae hae ta'en it at a'.
It fell frae her haun' and it rolled on the grun',
And it went through a hole in the wa'.

Chorus
*Did ye find a red Yo-Yo, red Yo-Yo, red Yo-Yo,*
*Did ye find a red Yo-Yo wi' a wee yellow string?*

The daring young Annie, she went tae the Janny,
A decent wee man as a rule.
It's pleasing to tell that he rang on his bell,
And he asked every wean in the school.

The weans left their pencils and papers and stencils
Tae knock on the doors all aroon';
And as they were rapping and ringing and chapping,
They asked a' the folk o' the toon.

The polis soon learned and they were concerned;
They left a' their murders aside.
The whole of the force was alerted of course,
And they went on the telly and cried.

156

All over the country, the common and gentry
Were watching their big T.V. screens.
Things really got gaun' some when President Johnson
Received an appeal frae the Queen.

The wires were tremblin' when he 'phoned the Kremlin
Tae ask aboot Annie's Yo-Yo.
But Kosygin agreed with the greatest of speed,
'Sio phonyo orchen strativichen,' (whatever it means).

In Peking and Paris and a' roon' the Barras,
The people they searched high and low,
Till finally Annie announced that her Granny
Had bought her another Yo-Yo.

Final Chorus
*And it was a red Yo-Yo, red Yo-Yo, red Yo-Yo,*
*It was a red Yo-Yo wi' a wee yellow string.*

# RICH MAN'S PARADISE

Chorus
*Rich man's paradise, poor man's hell,*
*Rich man's paradise, I bid fare-thee-well.*
*Bread and roses all the way, for the chosen few,*
*You ain't thinkin' of me my friend, but I'll be thinkin' of you.*

There is no pity, down in the city,
The gentlemen with heads held high,
Won't see the homeless lady, with a little homeless baby,
Little tears came glistening in his eyes.

Shipyard towns are dying, shipyard folk are crying,
Fearful of the things being done,
They won't hear them wailing, you will find them sailing,
With their 'Morning Clouds' they'll hide the golden sun.

When Sunday bells are ringing, you will hear them singing,
Songs of Praise, the Lord on high,
They will read the Lesson, call down Heaven's blessing,
Living through their Sunday morning lie.

# A RIGHT PROPER BAR STEWARD

Tune: *My Bonnie Lies Over the Ocean*

He worked on the boats as a steward
As a steward in one of the bars
And he was a proper bar steward
To all of the other Jack Tars

Chorus
*They sang bar steward bar steward*
*A right proper bar steward was he was he*
*Bar steward bar steward*
*A right proper bar steward was he*

He served them all short measured whisky
All the time he was at sea
One held up his glass and he pointed
'Behold in my glass floats a flea'

Said the steward, 'So what's so unusual?
Can you not let that little flea pass?'
Said he, 'It's the first flea that I've seen afloat
And touching the foot of the glass'

He'd worked on the boats as a steward
Almost the whole of his life
He knew how to pour gin and tonic
And where to place each fork and knife

# ROB ROY MACGREEGOR-O

Tune: *Duncan Gray*

Who's the cause o' a' the mirth,
Rob Roy MacGreegor-O,
Frae Glasgow Cross tae the Solway Firth,
Rob Roy MacGreegor-O.

Chorus
*Eat the breid an' heid the ba',*
*The man that ate the bile't ham raw,*
*He verra seldom kicked his maw,*
*Rob Roy MacGreegor-O.*

On a dainty sandwich he's gey keen
Two loaves o' breid an' a pig between.

When tae the dancin' he has gane
He aye leaves fourteen lassies hame.

Who puts on size 15 shoes
Drinks a barrel o' the rye-buck booze.

Who will right Auld Scotia's wrongs
Who is the leader o' the Tongs.

He never ever sings a song
Unless it's a hundred verses long.

That wis a real wee rotten verse
This one here is ten times worse.

At London toon he had a look
Kiss'd the Queen and chased the Duke

Frae Partick Cross up tae the Tron
Who knows every pub an' pawn.

# ROSY ANNA

Let the drunkard have his whisky,
The fiend can have his dope,
Let the miser have his money
And the hangman have his rope
*Give me Rosy Anna, Rosy Anna,*
*All day long I'm pining for my Rosy Anna.*

Let the farmer have his harvest
And the bar-fly have a pub,
Let the gambler have his flutter
And the glutton have his grub

The sheikh can have his harem
Of a hundred, two or three,
Give me my Rosy Anna
She's the only one for me

You can search the whole world over,
From Boston to Bengal,
But you'll have to come to Ru'glen
For the fairest of them all

F

# RU'GLEN JEAN

There's a lass called May, she comes from Inveraray,
There's a lass called Alice up in Aberdeen,
There's a Glesga Jessie all in competition,
But the one to have my heart to keep is Ru'glen Jean.

Chorus
*She has lips like crimson roses in the summer*
*And her eyes have the skies, her hair has got the sun.*
*She's as neat and sweet as I'm sure was ever fashioned,*
*And I'll guarantee she'll marry me before I'm done.*

There's a highland tang wi' the lass in Inveraray,
There's a touch o' spring wi' the lass in Aberdeen,
Wi' my Glesga Jessie there's the warmth o' the summer,
But you'll find them all together in my Ru'glen Jean.

I'll be tellin' May that's up in Inveraray,
I'll be tellin' Alice and Jessie and them all,
Go and find yourself another lad to centre your affections on,
And bring him to my weddin' in the big toon hall.

# RUM'LL HAE TO DAE THE DAY

Chorus
*Rum'll hae to dae the day and rid me o' my sorrow*
*Rum'll hae to dae the day and gin'll dae the morrow*

I donnered doon tae Ru'glen toon and there I met wi' Susan
She kissed me and she left me and 'twas that that set me boozin'

Now I've met another lass, her face is nice and bonnie
But I'm awful feart she wanders off and leaves me on my owny

I've just won a thousand pounds I'm awful feart I lose it
So just to rid me o' the fear I think I'd better booze it

The Ru'glen pubs are all shut doon tae celebrate the Sabbath
But I'll gang oot tae East Kilbride I aye make that my habit

They say that cider makes you thin and flighty as a feather
And whisky makes you awful fat so I'll hae baith together

# SKIN

Tune: *My Bonnie Lies Over the Ocean*

The cat has a lovely fur jacket,
The cow has a leather jerkin,
The sheep has a thick woollen jumper,
But we have got nothing but skin.

Chorus
*Skin, skin, skin, skin,*
*Nothing but skinny, skin, skin, skin, skin.*
*Skin, skin, skin, skin*
*Nothing but skinny, skin, skin.*

On the very last day of creation,
Nature had emptied her bin,
She ran out of clothes for her creatures,
And she turned us all out in our skin.

We were last in the queue at creation,
The others all did very well.
The birds commandeered all the feathers,
The tortoise flew off with the shell.

The leathers and hides of the others
Are far more effective than skin,
It doesn't protect you from weather,
It's simply for keeping you in.

Skin is quite good for complexion,
It's handy if you wish to blush,
So please treat your skin with affection,
Without it you're nothing but MUSH

With Crimplene and Orlon and Nylon
With silk and with serge and sat-in,
Please do your best to keep hidden,
The terrible scourge of the skin.

Some people really don't like it,
They'd chuck the lot in the bin,
Each time they turn on the telly
They can see nothing but skin.

Some folk are friendly some hostile,
You'll tell them from how they begin,
The foe will say 'gimme some money,'
A friend will say, 'gimme some skin.'

# SNOWFALL

Chorus
*When there is a snowfall*
*Gonna make a snowball*
*Gonna make a snowman too*
*With silver bells aringing*
*You will hear me singing*
*I'll be coming round for you*

Summertime is gone now
Winter coming on now
Father Christmas on his way
All I need to cheer me
Is my true lover near me
Then I'm gonna sing and say

When I make my snowman
Gonna make him go man
What a mighty man he'll be
He'll go climbing up the mountain
Walking in the valley
Sailing on the deep blue sea

With our little snowman
You and me can go an'
We'll be little snowmen too
Climbing and awalking
Sailing and atalking
Singing all the winter through

# STORNOWAY ROSE

There is a cavern of gold,
In the Cuillins of Skye,
Where riches and wealth untold,
Stand seven foot high.

Chorus
*So bid farewell my Love,*
*For time quickly flows,*
*Come over the Minch with me,*
*My Stornoway Rose.*

Away with your cavern of gold,
For I have heard tell,
Your Cullins gold my Love,
Is bound by a spell.

I've heard them say my Love,
Your sweet precious gold,
Can be had by any man,
For the price of his soul.

Treasures abound my Love,
In the Island of Skye,
I need no bribe of gold,
To the Cuillins I'll fly.

There is a cavern of gold,
In the Cuillins of Skye,
Where riches and wealth untold,
Stand seven foot high.

167

# TELL ME WHAT THE TEA LEAVES TELL ME

Chorus
*Tell me what the tea leaves tell me*
*Tell me Mumma do*
*Do they say that I will be*
*As lovely Mum as you*
*Do they say that I will marry*
*Or that I will have to tarry*
*Tell me what the tea leaves tell me*
*Tell me Mumma do*

My pretty little dolly wants to sit up here by me
And hear the lovely stories that you tell us from the tea
Of little bears and rabbits and their tricky little habits
Tell me what the tea leaves tell me tell me Mumma do

Of these pretty little stories I can never have enough
Tell me of the piggies and the wolf who went puff puff
Tell me all of those and then tell me all of those again
Tell me what the tea leaves tell me tell me Mumma do

Daughter darling daughter I will tell these tales to you
Tho' you know darling daughter they are sometimes not quite true
But I can never read your cup while all those leaves are covered up
So drink up darling daughter and I'll tell those tales to you

# THREE NIGHTS AND A SUNDAY

Chorus
*Three nights and a Sunday double time.*
*Three nights and a Sunday double time.*
*I work a' day and I work a' night,*
*Tae hell wi' you Jack, I'm all right.*
*Three nights and a Sunday double time.*

There's a fella doon the road that I avoid,
He's wan o' them they call the unemployed.
He says it's all because of me,
He canny get a job and I've got three.
Three nights and a Sunday double time.

The wife came tae the work the ither day.
Says she 'We've anither wee one on the way.'
Says I 'No wonder you can laugh,
I've no' been hame for a year and a half.'
Three nights and a Sunday double time.

I never miss the pub on a Friday night.
And there you'll always find me gay and bright.
You'll see me down at the Old Bay Horse,
I'm a weekend waiter there of course.
Three nights and a Sunday double time.

There's some will head for heaven when they die,
Tae find a Dunlopillo in the sky.
But I'll be going to the ither place,
For an idle life I couldny face.
Three nights and a Sunday double time.

G

# THE WEE KIRKCUDBRIGHT CENTIPEDE

The Wee Kirkcudbright Centipede
She was very sweet,
She was ever so proud of every
One of her hundred feet.
Early every morning,
Her neighbours came to glance,
She always entertained them
With a beautiful little dance.

Chorus
*As leg number ninety four*
*Gave ninety five a shunt,*
*Legs number one and two*
*Were twistin' out in front,*
*As legs numbers nine and ten*
*Were wriggling up the side,*
*Legs seventy three and four*
*Were doing the Palais Glide.*

Her neighbour Jenny Longlegs
With jealousy was mad
She went out and bought herself
A pencil and a pad.
She came a month of mornings
And made a careful note
Of every step the centipede made
And this is what she wrote.

Armed with exact notation,
Young Jenny Longlegs tried
To dance just like the centipede,
She failed and nearly cried,
She grabbed a hold of the centipede,
She says, 'Now have a look
And tell me how you do these steps
I've written in my book?'

Said the centipede, 'Do I do that?'
And she tried to demonstrate,
She'd never thought on the thing before
She got into a terrible state,
Her hundred legs were twisted,
She got tied up in a fankle,
She fractured seven shinbones
Fourteen kneecaps and an ankle.

As legs number one and two
Were tied to three and four,
Legs number five and six
Were trampled on the floor,
Leg number fifteen
Was attacked by number ten,
Ninety seven and ninety eight
Will never dance again.

The Wee Kirkcudbright Centipede,
She suffered terrible pain,
And some of us were very surprised
She ever danced again,
But now she tells her neighbours
Every one that calls to see,
Never try an explanation
Of what comes naturally.

# THE WELDER SONG

I never can hear the horn go blow
I never can see that big grey wall.
I pay nae heed to the gaffer at all,
For I aye hae my mind on you.

I'm weldin' steel from morning till night
They say my rod's aye burning bright.
I wouldna know if it's wrong or right,
For I aye hae my mind on you.

Of all the queens the Clyde has gi'en
To rule upon the brine,
It never gi'ed a fairer queen
Than the one that's on my mind.

# WE'LL HAVE A MAY DAY

Chorus
*We'll have a May Day My O My O We'll have a May Day then.*
*We'll have a May Day My O My O We'll have a May Day then.*

I have friends in London Town, the finest ever seen,
And I have some in Swansea and I've some in Aberdeen,
We're all Labour good and true, and I'll tell you what we're going to do,
We're going to fight this fight right through and we'll have a May Day then.

Back in '45 they marched, from barrack room and mill,
Determined they would make a change, for they had had their fill.
From the kitchen sink and coal they came, every Labour man and dame,
And shortly we'll be doing the same and we'll have a May Day then.

Our faithers fought this fight before, and thought that they had won,
You should have seen the boss turn green and how that man could run.
But when our faithers turned their backs, the boss came again to dodge his t
But the next time we'll no be so lax, and we'll have a May Day then.

They're never ever satisfied, though millions they have made,
But still they think that you and I are grossly overpaid,
There's nothing that they widnae steal, they even grudge your kids a meal,
But very soon you'll hear them squeal and we'll have a May Day then.

We'll join in jubilation and the big brass band you'll hear,
As we march on in triumph to the future with a cheer,
But as we greet the newborn day, the piper he'll have a tune to play –
A lament for the sharks that are on their way and we'll have a May Day then

H

# WITH FIRE AND WITH SWORD

Chorus
*With fire and with sword, Amen, Amen*
*With fire and with sword, Amen*
*With fire and with sword, here come the men of war,*
*Ah, the world must be coming to an end.*

They massacre the young, Amen, Amen,
They massacre the young, Amen,
They massacre the young, to make them hold their tongue,
Ah the world must be coming to an end.

There's blood upon their hands, Amen, Amen,
There's blood upon their hands, Amen,
There's blood upon their hands,
On this and other lands,
Ah the world must be coming to an end.

With their bayonets and their bombs, Amen, Amen,
With their bayonets and their bombs, Amen,
With their bayonets and their bombs, they'll be tearing down our homes,
Ah the world must be coming to an end.

Oh will they have their way, Amen, Amen,
Oh will they have their way, Amen,
Oh will they have their way, or will the young folks say,
That the world will not be coming to an end.

# YOU CANNAE KICK AROOND

**Chorus**

*You cannae kick around here,*
*Naw you cannae kick aroond here.*
*You cannae kick aroond here,*
*Naw you cannae kick aroond here.*
*You cannae, cannae, cannae,*
*You couldnae kick your grannie,*
*You cannae, cannae, cannae,*
*You cannae kick aroond here.*

When I was just a laddie
I went and asked my maw
If I could have a tanner
To buy a tanner ba'.
The tanner ba' she gave me
And I went oot tae play
But everywhere I took it
I heard the polis say:

Then I played for the Rovers
And I felt very proud
When I rushed up the centre
You should've heard the crowd
I'd make a shoot for goal
And you'd hear them roar and cheer
Then the ba' went past the post
And this was what you'd hear:

Ma fitba' days are over
And I'll be playin' nae mair
I had tae see the doctor
Because ma legs was sair
He tried some embrication
And gie'd ma leg a rub
Then, says he, You'd better go
And buy yersel a pub, because:

# Stories

# SAMSON

As you know, in Scotland, we have the highest standard of education in the world.

This is a fact which is universally acknowledged, and admitted as well, in places as far apart as Kirkcaldy and Carnoustie – it's even admitted in Kirkcudbright. And you know, I am well qualified to talk on this matter because I am the only man in Britain who ever taught English through an interpreter – and one day, there I was dealing with the children, you know, preparing them for their Z levels – when this Inspector came in to see if I was doing my job, you see.

And he said, 'Mr McGinn, have you been doing your job?' And Ah says, 'You ask the weans. Any question you like, you'll see Ah've been daein' ma job.' So he said to this wee boy, 'I want you to tell me – who was it who put his hands around the pillars and pulled them till the roof of the Temple crushed?' The wee boy says, 'Look it wisnae me. Ah was in the hoose a' last night. Cannae blame me.' So he says, 'What goes, Mr. McGinn?' Ah says – 'Well, if wee Jimmy says he didnae dae it –?' Naw, a good wee boy he was. Ah knew him very well. He widnae tell a lie.

So – 'Oh,' he says, 'Ah'll have to take this to the Headmaster.' Ah says, 'Ah'll go wae ye tae the Headmaster', ye see? So we went to the Headmaster and explained tae him. So the Headmaster, a very decent man, he says, 'Well Mr McGinn's been with us a very long time. Five weeks easy,' he says, 'and he's got a very good understanding of children,' and he says, 'If he thinks the boy didnae dae it–?'

So he still wisnae satisfied, this man, ye see? So he took it to the Education Committee, Lanarkshire Education Committee, ye see? So they, after he'd explained it to them, they locked themselves up wi' a couple of bottles of whisky, in behind, ye know? And they had a talk about it. And later the Chairman came out and says to this Inspector, he says, 'Look Mr Inspector,' he says, 'we've discussed this, and talked about it, and deliberated upon it, and everything', he says, 'and if you're prepared to forget all about this, we'll send round two bricklayers in the morning and get the whole thing fixed up.'

# THE SILVER SCREW

It is my painful, sad, sorrowful, woeful, but nonetheless hopefully profitable and certainly patriotic duty to relate, unfold and reveal to you and through you yours the diabolical and doubly devilish story of the dreadful misfortunes which befell a young Scottish boy.

For starters he was born right outside Glasgow.

But dear reader, spare your tears for even greater sorrow than being born outside the cradle of civilisation for believe you me or believe you me not there was even worse to follow.

His birth was a relatively peaceful and calm affair and the moment he was delivered his loving and adoring mother, who was a poor widow who had been for years, heaved a sigh of relief, lit a Woodbine and said, 'Thank heavens for that,' proceeding to puff peacefully at the fag.

This peace however was not to last long and was rudely broken by a cry of anguish from the attending doctor whose thin-lipped mouth involuntarily opened as he examined closely the child he had just helped bring into the world.

'Aaaaach!' he cried, stepping back from the infant.

'What's . . . the . . . matter?' said the widow, taking a puff of her Woodbine after each word.

'This wean hasnae got a belly button,' said the horror-stricken physician, picking up from the well-linoed floor the spectacles which had fallen from his long, thin, and at this moment, whitened face.

'What will I do, what will I do?' said the woman twice because she was anxious, and besides she had a stammer. 'In my professional opinion you had better have that child put down immediately,' said the medicine man who was a well known Partick Thistle supporter, 'Jags Jags Jags all the way.' 'No no no no,' insisted the widow because she had originally come from Glasgow, a city which is universally recognised as a place where they don't like having their children put down on a Tuesday which is the Half

Day closing day. 'No no no,' she said and had another puff of her cigarette adamantly.

'You cannae have a wean going through the world without a belly button. Think of the neighbours. What will they not say?' muttered the doctor, compassionately.

'No. I'll protect him. I'll hide the shame of it,' retorted the widow and so saying she stubbed out the cigarette end she had latterly been smoking with the aid of a pin, flung herself from the bed, pushed the doctor from the room and closed the door behind him and the bag which she had thrown after him.

Having so done she picked up the baby and proceeded to wrap him in the finest linen which only two days before she had been busily and feverishly shoplifting.

'I'll protect you son.' She almost sang 'I'll . . . ' Suddenly her mouth too was stuck open as she noticed that on the peak of the boy's pink belly where his umbilical cord should have been there was, glinting in the filtering sunlight, a tiny silver screw.

'Oh my God,' she said on recovering her composure. 'I'd better go to Edinburgh.'

From newspaper reports, history books and from stories which had strained their way through to the West she knew that the Capital city was one in which strange things occur. 'There must be millions of people running around Edinburgh with silver screws in place of belly buttons,' she said aloud to the child who had little understanding of the fuss that was being made over him and could offer no resistance as his mother rushed him through the streets, on the train and up the steps of Waverley Station to make discreet inquiries in the middle of Princes Street, where she could find no satisfactory reply to her questioning of would-be passers by.

'Excuse me,' she asked, stopping one after another of the lieges. 'Do you happen to have a silver screw instead of a belly button?'

Her knowledge of the Edinburgh folk was limited or she would have known that whether they had silver screws or belly buttons they would never have let on.

However, in Edinburgh she stayed to raise the unfortunate child, taking great care to conceal his affliction.

On sending him to school she always endearingly affixed a piece of sticking plaster over the offending screw so that if he were being given physical jerks or swimming lessons the other children would say, 'He's cut his belly again,' and assume that the boy's belly was accident prone, like a lot of the women in Edinburgh and for that matter in Glasgow.

Thus with great love and affection she brought him up to be a decent well-mannered youth whom everybody thought quite normal.

In fact it was not unusual for small knots of people to gather in Morningside and point him out with such remarks as 'Now doesn't he look quite normal.'

In this way he might well have gone through life with no one else knowing his deformity had not the biological urge taken the most dreadful grip of him at the age of eighteen.

This powerful biological urge caused him to eat and drink and even worse to take a fancy to a girl whom he eventually married.

On his wedding night he was lying in bed naked waiting for his bride when she entered and spotted the silver screw and immediately began to giggle.

Three times she giggled, giggle, giggle, giggle, and then she died which was not a nice thing to do on such a night. She could have waited for a more opportune moment.

However, as a result of this calamity he developed the most awful complex about his belly and went to see doctors and ministers and priests and rabbis and eventually the polis, who phoned up Interpolis who sent a bunch of flowers but who could do little else to assist him in his plight.
'Help me help me,' he was callling over and again as he left the polis office at the door of which he was approached by a Gypsy woman who had heard his pleas.

'Cross my palm with a half a quid,' she said and he gladly did.

From somewhere in the folds of her brightly and variously coloured skirt she brought forth a miniature crystal ball into which she gazed for two minutes before calling out to him, 'Go ye forth into the forest of Kirkcudbright on the night of the first full moon. Take off your clothes, lie down on the ground and look up at the moon.'

It being the month of November, the thought of lying naked in the middle of the night in Kirkcudbright he did not particularly enjoy.

But in his predicament he had little alternative but to rush down to the appointed forest, it being the night of the first full moon.

Naked, he lay down in a clearing, and looked up to discover there was no moon, it being very cloudy.

For four hours the unfortunate young man lay wriggling and writhing until he was just about to give up hope.

In fact, at this point he turned to me saying, 'I am just about to give up hope.'

But suddenly there developed a hole in the clouds and through this came a moonbeam which directed itself on to his silver screw.

He became very excited as all the forest lit up and even more ecstatic when dancing down the moonbeam came a tiny silver screw driver which inserted itself into the screw and turned the latter round eighteen and a half times.

Then screw and screwdriver went gaily dancing up the moonbeam in behind the clouds and out of sight.

The young man's mind was a symphony of joy. He gave a shout for joy, called out, 'God bless the Gypsy woman,' stood up and his bum fell off.

# THE FORTUNES OF FOGGY McGUFF

The nickname 'Foggy' was one which John McGuff had picked up as a boy, long before the swollen labour market of pre-war days, and a suspension from the Labour Exchange for what was called 'not genuinely seeking work,' caused him to embark on his back-court singing career. The nom-de-plume therefore was in no way connected with his tone of voice, which did, however, unfortunately resemble a foghorn.

The first sixteen days of his remarkable career were by far the most painful he had ever had to endure. He didn't earn a single penny, and, the moment he would enter the back court and open up with something like

Hu-wyeedidernju ma-ha-yake mercuhairr-uh . . .

one window after another would go down, until eventually he would be left singing to a blank wall. This was discouraging. His one consolation, in fact, during these sixteen days, was that in a certain pend in the Gallowgate there was a very pleasant-faced, middle-aged woman, who never closed her window upon him, and always threw him over a parcel of brown bread and cheese. Well, the cheese resembled Gorgonzola, which had never been Foggy's favourite, but it was sustaining, and besides that it was gratifying to think as Foggy did think until the sixteenth day, that here at least he had a fan.

However, on the sixteenth day, being particularly hungry, and grateful for the sandwich, he asked a wee boy who was standing in the back-court laughing at him, 'Would ye tell that woman thanks and God bless her.' Whereupon the wee boy says, 'Who? Mrs McKendrick? She's stone deif!'

Well, the blow was more than even the most modest man could endure, and Foggy left the back-court with the half-eaten sandwich crushed between his fingers, and tears trickling down the side of his nose.

A lesser man would have given the whole thing up there and then, but it was then that Foggy decided he would try dancing, and with the aid of a very generous publican in the area – there *was* one at that time – he obtained a wooden box and some beer-bottle tin-tops – tinnies – which he fastened to the soles of his shoes, and for four days he toured the area, giving a very commendable performance of what became known locally as 'The Tin-Shoe Shuffle.' Now, this proved very popular, in particular with the children, who followed him in their hundreds. Even so, there was no money forthcoming. Certainly, there were other things. For example, there was the half of a cabbage, which Foggy thoroughly enjoyed, but the ferocity of its fall from a two-storey window, and the mark which it left on Foggy's nose, didn't exactly endear him to its donor. He certainly didn't want him to form a fan club. Besides this, there were eggs, but these, he could tell, as they fell on and around his platform, had lain a wee bit too long to be wholesome. However, they constituted a promise for the future, and on that basis Foggy would have been prepared to continue, had it not been for his varicose veins. As a result of these he collapsed, while in the middle of a performance, to be carried home to his house in the Calton by a scavenger who had nipped into the back-court for a smoke.

In his house in the Calton Foggy would have died, in the first place of hunger, and in the second place of despair, had it not been for that fateful factor's letter. He'd been getting these letters from MacFadyen for a long time, and recognised the envelope the moment it arrived. He says, 'That's fae MacFadyen!' and, thinking it ridiculous that a man with money like MacFadyen had, should be sending begging letters to an unfortunate character like himself, he threw it on the mantlepiece, where it would have lain, gathering dust along with the rest, had it not been for the extreme cold of the following day. It was so cold that Foggy took the momentous decision to light a fire. It was momentous in the circumstances, because of course Foggy had no coal, no sticks, no paper. However, having stuffed the grate with his last bit of linoleum, Foggy lifted the letter from the mantlepiece, to get a light from the stair-head gas, and – heaven knows what made him do it, but he suddenly decided to have a look at this letter. And it was a good job he did, because this was not in the ordinary run of begging letters from MacFadyen. This was an outright ultimatum that he'd either have to cough up or get out. Well, he did cough – and splutter – and flew out in a heedless panic, wondering to himself who he could turn to, who he could tap; there was nobody. He'd tapped everybody.

However, he suddenly began to ask himself: Who, why, what is responsible for all this? Even more suddenly, it hit him like a bolt, that it was the Orangemen. Suddenly he could see that behind every one of the closed windows, the eggs and the cabbage, there stood an Orangeman, who was trying to persecute him because his name was Foggy McGuff. With this, he went blind with rage and he rushed into a back-court in the Calton.

Had he not been blind with rage he could have seen that it was a Celtic supporter's back-court, you know, with the yellow curtains and the green curtains, but as I say, blind with rage he faced up to the windows and he says, 'Well, I might be down and done for but by God I'll show them the sort of stuff Foggy McGuff's made of.' So he opens up with 'Faith of Our Fathers'. . .

Faieeuthuvva Fazziayuhzzer . . .

Well, the people in the houses were horrified at the voice, but they began to ask themselves would it not maybe be sacrilege to close down the window on a hymn like that – maybe we'd better ask the priest if we can close the window on a thing like that. Well, Foggy saw the open windows, and he interpreted these as a sign of the ordinary cowardice of Orangemen, whereupon he decided to double the challenge with the 'Irish Soldier's Song.' Even so, they didn't want to throw him over money, in case it would encourage him back, but they held their windows open. But when Foggy decided to move from that to 'O Salutaris' . . .

Oooooo-wah Sal-yuha-tarrisherzaber . . .

they decided individually and en masse that something would need to be done. It was then that they began throwing him ha'pennies and pennies and threepenny bits. Foggy jumped about the back-court collecting them, going, 'God Bless Ye, God Bless Ye,' you know, and he picked up 14/3½d — all in one back-court. He was quite softened by this, you know, and he says, 'Even though they're Orangemen,' and gave them a non-Party tune — but before he reached the third note of 'The Last Rose of Summer' every window in the place was closed down.

However, it was a different Foggy McGuff that left that back-court. That day he visited nineteen similar back-courts in the Calton, and collected £4/19/2¾d, plus a large number of foreign coins (from which he was able to deduce that there was a big Norwegian colony in the area). From that day onward he never looked back. He picked up the tricks of the back-court trade — he learned the words of 'The Old Orange Flute' and 'The Protestant Boys', which enabled him to undertake work in the Dalmarnock area, which was infested with Rangers supporters. By singing a suitable song in each place he eventually made a fortune and today he owns a string of picture halls in the Liverpool area.

Regarding his former background he very seldom talks, and in fact he would have forgotten about it, had it not been for his charred finger-tips. These he received at the hands of a renegade Orangeman, who had inveigled his way into a house in the Ham building, through the medium of a mixed marriage. For spite this customer, who had apparently lost the love he formerly had for his wife, used to roast pennies over the gas and throw them out at Foggy. These made Foggy jump so high that on one occasion there was a woman three stairs up who had him arrested as a Peeping Tom. In spite of all this, Foggy holds no bitterness, and it is his hope that one day he will be able to retire, and, to show that he has no bitterness, return to Glasgow, and stand outside Ibrox Park, Rangers end, when Rangers are playing at home, and distribute half-crowns — from a chestnut barrow.

# THE MISDEEDS OF SYLVESTER McQUIGLEY

## INTRODUCING
## SYLVESTER McQUIGLEY

Sylvester McQuigley was no angel. On that we will readily agree. But to suggest that he was an entirely evil man as do certain well-informed persons is to paint a false picture which can only serve to misguide the recorders of history who have striven so hard in the past to give us an account of our heritage and traditions but who have been hindered so often in their noble endeavour by such people who do not believe what they see, so much as see what they believe. It is in order to offset any possible error which should otherwise arise from this malignant source that we present to the public this untarnished and objective account of what have been described as the misdeeds of Sylvester McQuigley.

McQuigley was born the seventh son and eleventh child of poor but dishonest parents in a single end in the lower part of Glasgow's Gallowgate. His father Josiah was an unsuccessful hawker of Irish Hebrew origin who had chosen this particular abode partly because he considered· it a suitable environment in which to rear his eleven sons and daughters and partly because he had no alternative.

The house itself was of sound construction, the builders having gone to considerable trouble to transport from the outlying districts substantial quantities of brick and timber. So good indeed was the workmanship that it had been enabled to withstand for two centuries and more, the worst rigours of the Clydeside weather. So much so that even after a heavy shower of rain there were no floods and only an occasional leak in the bed recess.

Running water was laid on, which was a considerable improvement in the provision enjoyed by Josiah McQuigley's forefathers in that little village outside Jerusalem which they had left only five thousand years prior to the birth of Sylvester.

For purposes of sanitation the McQuigleys did not have to travel far, there being provided for their convenience a water closet which they enjoyed in common with the other four families on the landing.

Thus, in comfort and with lavish helpings of oatmeal and herring, did Sylvester spend his infancy.

Already, in early childhood, he had begun to display the truly astounding talents which have led to his erstwhile infamy and which made his name a household word among the other families on the landing and, indeed, throughout the length and breadth of the Pickle pend. The first of these to become apparent was the astonishing rapidity with which he could pick things up.

So well developed was this particular talent that it might well have gone unnoticed, had it not been for the exceptional vigilance of a certain store detective in the centre of the city. Once, however, it had been observed, it became clear that the boy was too far advanced for any ordinary school. With a view therefore to the further development of his talents, he was transferred to a more advanced type of educational establishment without delay, and in great haste. To a school in fact which had been properly approved by the appropriate authority. Let it be said the foremost authority in the country!

The particular college in which he was thereby installed was in the charge of a certain religious organisation which held the belief, among others, that the full fruit of man's wisdom, knowledge and morality could be best imparted to the scholar through the medium of benevolence and generosity. To this end the teachers were specifically issued with instructions to avoid, where possible, the drawing of blood from the hides of the students. An instruction which was faithfully obeyed. So much so, that the students seldom required outside hospital treatment.

We give this brief account of the early background of Sylvester in order that the reader will be possessed of a fuller impression of his roots and his misdeeds and will thereby be enabled to make an unprejudiced judgement.

There is another important factor to which the reader's attention must be drawn. That is the religion which Sylvester adopted. This is an important entity in estimating the life, deeds and works of any man, or woman for that matter, and must of course be considered in any case of the present subject.

The adoption of a religion is an important question for any person as the reader will readily agree, but whereas the problem is easily overcome by most people, there being to hand in most homes some religion or other which the person easily accepts, good, bad or indifferent and without a great deal of bargaining or argumentation, it was somewhat complicated for Sylvester, as will be understood, and it was the one thing which ever caused him to lose sleep.

The complications arose from diverse sources. There was the fact that his father was an Irish Hebrew, himself somewhat confused, and his mother a hardened Scots Presbyterian with no sympathy with the idea of Bishops in the Kirk. And there was the example of his college superiors towards which Sylvester had somewhat mixed feelings.

It was therefore inevitable that the boy should grow into some kind of non-conformist or heathen. Having nothing but feelings of loathing and detestation for heathens, Sylvester chose non-conformity for he recognised that it was necessary to have some kind of religion to guide one through life. But the problem was one to which he had to devote a great deal of thought and mental energy, it being his desire not to be entangled with too many commandments.

After him giving the matter many days' consideration his problem was solved by a lecture it was his privilege to hear given by a certain famous Glasgow open air preacher. With only one hearing he was converted to a religion with an absolute minimum of do's and don'ts; in fact, with only one commandment. Namely that a man must at all times be good to his Granny and give her plenty of whiskey. The lecture filled Sylvester with great relief and induced him to make his one and only ever contribution to a public subscription. His donation, it must be noted, consisted of two French francs which he had picked up in Kent Street a fortnight before and which he had decided to keep as a souvenir. It will therefore be appreciated that in making the donation Sylvester was making a substantial sacrifice which rendered unwarrantable the avowed disapproval and rebuke of the preacher, who cursed and swore, thereby exposing himself as a blistering hypocrite with one interest in life, namely the gathering of funds.

Be that as it may, a creed cannot be condemned simply

through the malevolence of a person claiming adherence and Sylvester left the sneering preacher and hostile gathering feeling elated that he had at last found a religion he could embrace with his mind, body and soul and yet which did not prove too cumbersome to him in his misdeeds.

To this religion, as even hostile observers will testify, he has ever adhered. So that if the obedience of the commandments in which one believes be the criterion set at the Pearly Gates then assuredly Sylvester will have his place in the heavenly host, for, as the Gallowgate well knows, his Granny was never sober, and despite the claim of a generous National Assistance Board the responsibility lies with Sylvester McQuigley.

The last environmental factor which we will mention is one of no less importance. We refer to the wart which an inconsiderate nature had placed inconveniently on the point of his otherwise unobtrusive nose and which defied all the knowledge and experience of medical science. This was, as will be readily appreciated, a source of acute embarrassment to Sylvester and a distinguished feature which set the remainder of society with the sympathetic exception of his Granny against him, and led him to adopt his otherwise inappreciable standpoint of malevolence intermingled with an element of goodness of a kind.

With these remarks on his early environment, his love of his Granny, the wart on his nose and a reference to the fact that his great desire in life was to live with a minimum of physical effort, we introduce Sylvester McQuigley.

# THE DAY LABOURERS

On a certain windswept corner, in the vicinity of Glasgow Cross, was situated a stance for casual labourers. There, of a morning, would gather anything up to a hundred men old and young, muscular and puny, rosy and pale, anxious for a day's employment and ready to compete with one another for the jobs available.

From different parts of the city would emerge agents with orders for men, ready to hire the day labourers. But of course there were the slack periods when business was slow or at a standstill and on such occasions the men did not stand still long, for as we have said the corner was windswept and the unsuccessful competitors would make their way back to their respective homes or to the Labour Exchange, looking none too cheerful at the non-realisation of their ambitions.

Of a busy morning the agents would appear, pick their required number of men, take hold of their insurance books and direct them to their appropriate place of employment.

Things were slack on that fateful December morning in the winter of 1942 at the height of the World War when Sylvester McQuigley decided to become an employer of labour. Little did that group of twenty five men know what fate held for them as they stood ready and eager to engage in the war production drive. Their eagerness was reflected in their posture; there were congregated the last stalwarts of an original crowd of ninety five men the remainder of whom had taken to their heels with the information that things were slack and no jobs were available. The group were in eager mood, their hands inside their coats and jackets clutching their thighs and some even dancing with the sheer joy of life despite the cold and shower of sleet which drizzled in their cheerful faces regardless of whether these were clean shaven or bearded, as many were.

Despite a most interesting conversation on who had won the league in 1933 there were many who were on the verge of contemplating joining their departed comrades when a person easily distinguishable as an employer's agent by his soft hat, raincoat, glasses, a brown moustache and a neat piece of sticking plaster on his nose obviously covering a blemish caused by over-nourishment, appeared. There was a flurry of excitement as the aspirants pushed and shoved their way into more advantageous positions eager to attract the attention of the agent who curtly announced that he wanted twenty four men for a digging operation.

In a cultured voice he picked his men – You, You and You, he intoned, beckoning them to one side after pocketing their Insurance Books which they anxiously thrust into his uncalloused hands – 'And You and that's the lot,' he announced when he had left only one rather pitiful little man feeling out of it. The agent was ushering the others in the direction of the Gallowgate when, stricken with sympathy at the plight of the poor little man in whose throat a lump had appeared, he waved him to his side, 'Alright, you come along too.' A cheer arose from the others who were quick to appreciate the generosity of the gesture and of the agent who was prepared to hire an extra hand rather than cause human misery.

The little man was obviously possessed of a great knowledge of the English language for as the agent directed the twenty five men to a builder's yard in a sidestreet nearby he expressed in forty three different terminologies exactly how thankful he was for the agent's mercy and benevolence.

When they arrived at the builder's yard, which was little used these days, the agent explained to his men, due to the war-time restriction on certain building operations, the agent after fumbling in his pockets announced that 'Dash it all' he had forgotten his keys and that this would possibly mean the cancellation of the digging operation. With this announcement fear and panic swept the ranks of the labourers only to be relieved with the information proferred by a rather hungry-looking specimen who announced that he was very handy with a hairpin. The agent eyed him suspiciously but after consideration agreed that he should pick the lock. He was even more suspicious when the greasy-looking man produced the requisite pin from the pocket of an oil stained and well worn jacket.

This done, the enthusiastic labourers were issued with a pick and shovel each and after the hairpin man had secured the padlock once again, were directed by the agent to a spot on the Gallowgate which they readily agreed was badly in need of repair. The job, they were informed, was to lift the stones in an agreed area. With these instructions and a cheer from the men because a bonus would be paid if the job was well done, the agent left whistling a then-popular melody.

The men proceeded with the job in hand and some of them having had experience with this kind of work they made some very neat observations on exactly how many stones they would require to lift per hour in order to make the job spin out and allow them a sufficiency of spells in which to take it in turns to knock off for a smoke.

During these spells they had the opportunity for a discussion on all kinds of topics, ranging from football to horse racing, with a rather corpulent and ruddy-faced policeman who assisted in directing the traffic and even threw in a few hints on the most utilitarian methods of lifting and laying stones. The constable was a cheerful happy man and told them some very funny stories which made even one of their number, who was a regular breacher of the peace and had a certain dislike for the hand of the law, laugh. He even shared his sandwiches with the little hungry-looking man who wore a happy beaming smile throughout that livelong day feeling as he did that it was the happiest day he could remember.

Nor was their feeling of joy confined to the last men the agent had picked. The others could scarcely remember such a happy day's work with the steady drizzle of sleet and the fresh winds blowing from all directions into their cheerful faces making them feel clean, adding to the warm feeling that here they were being allowed to work without any arrogant foreman, in fact without any foreman breathing down their necks.

This latter point did cause a little trouble early on in the morning when one or two of their number, wishing to curry favour and with the idea that here in the absence of a foreman lay the possibility of cutting out a niche for themselves, did try and establish themselves as supervisors but they were quickly bludgeoned into place by the others who were democrats to boot – and didn't want any little Schicklegrubers emerging from their ranks.

The job, it must be recorded, was well done. Even the constable remarked on this fact and the stones were neatly packed by the side of the roadway. General satisfaction prevailed and the spells during the latter part of the day were enjoyed even more than in the morning for they felt that they really had been earned.

Occasionally, a passer-by would stop and express admiration for the way in which the job was being tackled and even exchange bits of gossip with the roadmen. The local inhabitants were delighted that at last that bit of the road was being tackled. It was, they explained, something of a miracle that there hadn't been an accident long before now with the state the road was in and it was disgraceful that some of the Councillors hadn't seen to it before now. Of course that was perfectly natural with the Councillors who forgot their civic duties the moment they were elected. Yes it was ridiculous. The roadmen nodded agreement with these comments, from which they learned a great deal about the work of the Corporation and about road repair and many other things.

Time passed rapidly and soon it was five o'clock with the roadmen feeling really satisfied with a day's work well done. They expected the agent to arrive any moment with their wages and their books duly stamped. Gradually their expectations gave way to a minor form of anxiety when the kind and generous agent didn't arrive with the goods. And of course he never did arrive for Sylvester had early on exchanged the Insurance Books for five pound notes.

Great indignation filled the Gallowgate when the news of the misdeed spread among the populace and of course suspicion centred upon Sylvester McQuigley. His enemies, who included everyone except as we have said his Granny, used the incident in order to raise the demand that he be exiled to the South Side or Partick and if it had not been for the shrewdness Sylvester McQuigley displayed in lying low for four days in his Granny's, something of the sort might have taken place. But of course with those four days emotions subsided and people were able to take a much cooler and less malicious viewpoint.

The realisation dawned that the deed was not so evil as at first imagined. It was true that Sylvester had handed the books to a certain black-marketeer who was only interested in making cash but they had found their way into the hands of twenty-five men who used them in order to engage in the great war production drive. So keen were those men to engage in this drive that they were prepared to defy military and naval authorities in order to get into indirect contact with Sylvester and thereby be enabled to place their energy in the essential production services.

Besides, when the casual labourers were interviewed by a reporter from the *Calton Clarion* they agreed that they had never done a more satisfying day's work. They had enjoyed immensely the fact that they did not have to endure the tyranny of a foreman criticising their every moment or immobility, and thereby initiated the campaign still being conducted by the *Clarion* for the dismissal of every foreman in the Clydeside for an experimental period of ten years.

There was also the fact that the incident made clear to the world the generosity of Glasgow policemen for the constable agreed not to arrest the twenty five men provided they replaced the stones. The replacement was completed before midnight when the grateful labourers expressed their thanks and bade farewell to the cheerful and highly sympathetic policeman, who, in any case, had been thankful for their company and expressed the hope that they would come again.

As for Sylvester he was able to secure a supply of spirits sufficient to keep his good old Granny fully occupied for seven weeks and this made him the happiest man in the Gallowgate.

# THE MEDICINAL WINE

A reputation is an easier thing to obtain than it is to be rid of. This fact has caused much unnecessary displeasure to many a person and establishment with good reason to wish to be relieved of some stigma of a bygone day. But of course it can also have its advantage. That is if the reputation is a good one which the person or establishment finds difficulty in continuing to justify.

Such is the position with a certain public house in the Partick area, the name of which we shall not mention for the very simple reason that any additional publicity might lead to the loss of the licence due to overcrowding, for already the proprietor finds difficulty in catering for the large clientele which flocks thereto from every corner of Glasgow and indeed the globe in search of a certain medicinal wine believed to be procurable therein.

The origin of the legend is an interesting one but in view of the great satisfaction obtained by many a person in every airt and pairt through the belief in the myth, we hope that the reader will take the story no further. We ourselves would never have divulged it but for the need for historical accuracy regarding Sylvester McQuigley. For as the reader will possibly have guessed, if he or she be above average intelligence, the wine, the legend and Sylvester McQuigley's misdeeds are closely associated.

There was a time during the war when Sylvester had a quarrel with his Granny. She quite justifiably accused him of drying up her supply of whiskey. He argued, quite correctly, that funds were low and in any case she had been drinking too heavily recently. Angry words were spoken and his Granny suggested that he should leave her house for a period in order that he should be taught a lesson. Sylvester, with a sad heart and a troubled conscience felt that the punishment was fair in view of this, his one and only breach of his religious beliefs, and removed himself.

He endeavoured unsuccessfully to find digs in the East End but failed for the simple reason that the people there know him like a bad ha'penny and they certainly know a bad ha'penny when they see one. He travelled further afield into the Gorbals, Govan and elsewhere but alas his reputation had preceded him and the doors were closed on Sylvester. It was then that he decided to try Partick and there he found shelter with an elderly widow who, be it known, was somewhat short-sighted and eccentric and insisted on the regular weekly payment of the rent.

He would have probably been happy in that area as his room window looked down upon the works gates of a number of factories and yards and thereby afforded a worthwhile view of thousands of men and women going to and from their work. This would have given him many a pleasurable hour as he had always, since he was very young, liked to see men going to their work, but unfortunately there were those in the vicinity who had other ideas. We refer to a number of Broo Clerks in the area who had received a full report on Sylvester, seeing as how he had to transfer to their Exchange.

These evil schemers had prepared a plot which would force the unfortunate McQuigley into employment and thereby reduce taxation and assist in the war production drive.

It was a warm day in September when, as the Gallowgate man innocently entered the Exchange unsuspecting and whistling one of his Granny's favourite tunes, hell broke loose. The four clerks vaulted the counter and thrust handcuffs on their unfortunate victim who was then carried bodily and screaming, 'I'm no the only wan!' which in any case was perfectly irrelevant and buttered no toast with the berserk clerks who were only interested in keeping the labour market supported.

Understandably attracting the attention of the local populace who rent the air with a great cheer when they learned the identity of the captive, Sylvester was thus transported to a public house nearby. The same public house referred to above.

Shaking the sawdust from his clothes, he was placed in the hands of the burly chargehand whose shortage of labour was in no way attributable to the fact that he paid the lowest wages in the district, although he did. The burly barman was much more pleased than was Sylvester with the contract of labour which was then enacted.

McQuigley was to be employed as a cellarman, barman, room-tender, sweeper-up, bottlewasher and odd job man, and the chargehand assured him that as long as he kept good time, did his work and everything he was told, he in turn would repay him by not lifting his hand too often. This was at least a consolation but even so, Sylvester was unhappy and miserable and wished he was back with his Granny. But all his pleadings with the burly barman were to no avail. The contract was struck and couldn't be broken – or so said the barman.

But of course the indomitable Gallowgate man was not to accept defeat so readily and soon he recovered from the severe shock of his abduction, and his brain, which was the only organ in his body which had ever worked until then, was quite soon active and like the genius he was he concluded that the barman must be induced into a dismissal.

He decided he would try being lazy. This effort gave him little trouble as in any case he was a person inclined towards leisure and it first appeared that he was meeting with success as he lounged around the bar and the chargehand gave him many an angry look hoping that this would be sufficient to scare the unfortunate Sylvester into some kind of activity. He would of course have taken a much sterner attitude had his custom and clientele which already stood at a very low ebb been thereby reduced. But the strange turn of events was that the clientele increased. This was because the pub began to take on the appearance of a real lounge which was an improvement in those days of continuous hurly burly and excitement. The pub attracted hundreds of sufferers from stomach ulcers who enjoyed the leisurely spectacle of the lazy waiter, and the barman grew pleased and smiled on his protegé.

Sylvester decided on a change of tactics and his next idea was stimulated strangely enough while waiting for a car one evening when his toil was over. He noticed a car travelling westward with the indicator informing the public that it was headed for a district near Partick known as Whiteinch. It struck a bell and he decided on his next manoeuvre, the whiteinch.

Until then the procedure for pouring the beer was simple enough. The measure was filled to the brim with beer and topped outside of the glass with a thick rich froth which could be scooped off with a stick provided for the purpose. Sylvester altered the position so that the froth became part of the pint, the actual beer ending one inch from the brim. The remainder became known as the whiteinch.

But alas, this effort proved futile. For few of the customers took any notice of the innovation and, of those who did, some were sufficiently patriotic to attribute it to some new wartime restriction which one must naturally accept in the interests of victory, while others who might have complained took note of the burliness of the chargehand and held their tongues. There was also the fact that the takings increased. For the saving of an inch a pint amounted to a barrel in a week and this pleased the chargehand who was quite struck by the ingenuity of Sylvester whose attempt to obtain the sack only ended in his being promoted to 'second hand' which meant he was now superior to the weekend man who was the only one to show displeasure at the whiteinch.

In desperation Sylvester tried watering the whiskey in order to drive off the custom and provoke the chargehand but he proved so expert at this that he was given the job steady. It was then Sylvester, in a fit of complete and utter despair, decided to have a consultation with a certain chemist acquaintance with a dispensary in the Plantation area.

Sylvester composed a cock and bull story for this chemist whom he had told he had a stable of forty five horses, all suffering from constipation. He asked his advice. The chemist was most sympathetic and only charged Sylvester eight shillings and tenpence for the two laxative bottles he concocted. Sylvester returned to the pub a much happier man and at the first opportunity dislodged the contents into three casks of wine.

His next step was to chalk up an 'Out of Order' sign on the toilet door and, in case any of the clientele were short sighted, to change the key which always hung behind the bar for one which closely resembled it but of course was not quite the thing. This done, he waited for the eruption and indeed an eruption there was, the like of which Partick has never seen.

Doctors were brought in from surrounding areas to deal with the epidemic and for some time panic prevailed during which the burly chargehand dismissed Sylvester for he thought there was something suspicious in the smirk he wore. Sylvester found his way back to the East End and his Granny, who welcomed him with open arms, agreeing that he had endured sufficient punishment.

As for the sufferers, they quickly recovered and from that day to this they have not uttered a single complaint and swear they never felt better, a fact which they attributed to the medicinal wine.

This then is the origin of the legend.

# BIBLIOGRAPHY

*Poems for Working Men*. Rutherglen: Matt McGinn, n.d.
*The Treasure Chest*. Glasgow: A. Thomson, [c. 1957].
*Scottish Songs of Today*. London: Harmony Music, 1964.
*Once Again Matt McGinn*. London: Heathside Music, 1970.
*Fry the Little Fishes*. London: Calder & Boyars 1975.
*The Big Effen Bee*. Glasgow: William MacLellan Embryo Books, 1976.
*Chapbook* Vol. 4, No. 4, 1967 (Special Matt McGinn Issue).
*Matt McGinn. The Treasure Chest*. IN Matt McGinn Collection, 1953.
*Matt McGinn. The Songs of Matt McGinn*, 1978.

# DISCOGRAPHY

*Honesty is out of the Fashion* (Xtra 1071)
*Little Ticks of Time* (Xtra 1078)
*Matt McGinn* (Xtra 1045)
*Matt McGinn Again* (Xtra 1057)
*Matt McGinn Sampler* (Transatlantic TRA SAM8)
*Screwtops are Falling on my Head* (Pye PKL 5527)
*Take me Back to the Jungle* (RCA INTS 1240)
*Tinny Can on my Tail* (RCA INTS 1368)
*The Two Heided Man* (Emerald Gem GES 1079)
*The Two Heided Man Strikes Again* (Emerald Gem GES 1120)
    Also featured on:
*Revival in Britain* Vol. 1 (Folkways FW8728)
*A Cold Wind Blows* (Elektra EUK-253)
*McGinn of the Calton*. The songs and stories of Matt McGinn presented by Stramash 1990 (1994) Greentrax Records (CD Trax 034) (stereo cassette)

Matt McGinn died on 6th January 1977 aged
48. With family and friends gathered, some of
his ashes were scattered on the grave of John
MacLean, Marxist teacher and Socialist
Republican, in Eastwood Cemetery on May Day
1977 and the remainder on the grass of
Glasgow Green by his widow Janette.